History of Christianity

An Enthralling Overview of the Most Important Events that Shaped the Christian Church

Free limited time bonus

Stop for a moment. We have a free bonus set up for you. The problem is this: we forget 90% of everything that we read after 7 days. Crazy fact, right? Here's the solution: we've created a printable, 1-page pdf summary for this book that you're reading now. All you have to do to get your free pdf summary is to go to the following website: **https://livetolearn.lpages.co/enthrallinghistory/**

Once you do, it will be intuitive. Enjoy, and thank you!

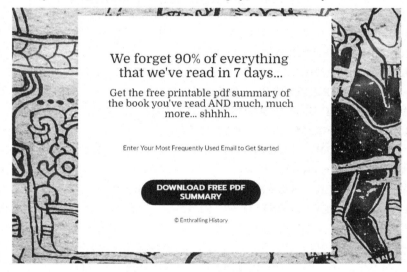

We forget 90% of everything that we've read in 7 days...

Get the free printable pdf summary of the book you've read AND much, much more... shhhh...

Enter Your Most Frequently Used Email to Get Started

DOWNLOAD FREE PDF SUMMARY

© Enthralling History

Table of Contents

Introduction: The Universal Appeal of the Christian Faith

A lot can be said about Christianity. Even if you are not a believer, Christianity is such a common feature of human culture in general that it is virtually inescapable. The fact that Christmas is the most popular holiday in the world is perhaps the most obvious testament to this fact.

Japan's percentage of practicing Christians is estimated to be less than 2 percent. However, the celebration of Christmas has been growing there for the past few decades. The holiday is just as eagerly celebrated in Japan as it would be in more traditionally Christian nations, such as the United Kingdom or the United States. It is pretty safe to say that no other religion can claim such universal global dominance in its influence.

This book documents the history of Christianity's historic rise, as well as how the religion has continued to influence humanity throughout the centuries. This book is not an attempt to make anyone a believer in the Christian faith; rather, it is an attempt to demonstrate the irrefutable impact that Christianity has had on the world.

Explore the days of Christ, the Council of Nicaea, the Reformation, and beyond. We will examine all of the incredible twists and turns of a faith born in the obscure desert town of Bethlehem and how it influenced world history.

PART ONE: The Origins of Christianity (1 CE–1100 CE)

Chapter 1: One Man and a Crucifix

As one might assume, Christianity ultimately began with Jesus Christ. There are perhaps some forerunners who could be mentioned, such as John the Baptist. John's ministry was similar to Jesus' ministry in that he called for a change in the spiritual order. John has also been linked to a community of spiritual enthusiasts eager for the end of the age. The group was known as the Essenes, and they endlessly prophesied about the coming of the "sons of light." The New Testament largely depicts John the Baptist as the one who passed the torch to Jesus, who ultimately was seen as the true Messiah.

In order to get to the roots of Christianity, we have to start with Jesus Christ himself. Since Christianity is such a well-known religion, most are familiar with the story. Jesus is said to have been the product of an immaculate conception and was birthed in a stable in Bethlehem. Historians are hesitant to believe much of the biblical narrative. There are even those who are skeptical that Jesus ever existed in the first place.

But since there are many sources outside of Christianity that talk about the existence of Christ, such an argument is pretty hard to make. Jesus is mentioned, at least in passing, by Roman historians. These Roman historians had no interest in becoming Christians and presented themselves as impartial observers. Although these few references are fleeting and lacking in great detail, they are important since they clearly demonstrate that Christ was known beyond the immediate Christian fold.

However, as it pertains to Christ's life, the only detailed work that remains is the Gospels. And when it comes to the Gospels, many consider the Gospel of Mark to be both the oldest (meaning it was written closest to the time of Christ's ministry on Earth) and the most accurate. There is some mention of a so-called hypothetical "Q" source, a missing piece of contemporary text that the writers of the Gospels used, but it has never been found.

The Gospel of Mark is probably the most accurate depiction of Jesus that the world currently has, as the other canonical Gospels were largely built off of Mark. It must be noted that the Gospel of Mark does not have much of the backstory of Christ, which is provided by the other Gospels. Instead, Mark focuses primarily on Christ's ministry, his death on the cross, and his resurrection.

So, to get a better idea of Jesus' birth in the manager or the traditional Christmas story, which features wise men, a stable in Bethlehem, and a newborn king, we need to turn to the other Gospels. Critics, of course, will try to suggest that the reason the events of the Christmas story were not included in the Gospel of Mark was that they did not happen.

However, such critics would have to contend with the fact that a prominent historian and contemporary of Jesus, a Jewish-Roman chronicler by the name of Josephus, compiled two whole scrolls on the life of Herod the Great. And within these scrolls, he listed an endless stream of atrocities committed by this most dastardly of dictators. Herod was indeed great, as he rebuilt the Jewish Temple and engaged in other massive building projects across the land, but according to Josephus, he had a dark side.

Although Josephus does not mention the slaughter of the innocents, he paints a picture of a man who would not hesitate to do such a thing. Josephus even chronicles an incident in which Herod, in one of his notorious outbursts, allegedly tried to lure a large group of prominent citizens from Israel into a stadium so he could slaughter them all. Even Roman Emperor Augustus (who was Herod's boss) spoke of Herod's callous disregard for life.

In consideration of how many of Herod's own children he had killed and due to various suspicions of other atrocities, Emperor

Augustus is said to have stated that he would "rather be Herod's pig than his son." In Greek, the words were more humorous since they rhymed, with Augustus saying that he would rather be Herod's *choiros* than his *huios.*

At any rate, according to the traditional Christmas narrative, after the three wise men from the East informed Herod of the portents of the star over Bethlehem, King Herod went berserk. He just could not countenance anyone being born that might outshine him, so he ruthlessly ordered all male children under two years of age to be killed. According to this account, he was so deranged that he would actually kill a bunch of innocent kids (hence the slaughter of the innocents) just to get at the newborn Christ.

This story is an incredible one, and skeptics understandably have a hard time believing such a brutal act occurred. But if we look at the examples presented by the non-Christian historian Josephus, it seems likely that King Herod was indeed capable of such a thing. So, it is clear that this one event mentioned in the Christmas story could have happened. Of course, the jury is still out as to whether or not it happened. There are many unanswered questions, such as whether Herod was even alive when Jesus was born or if this was a story that parallels Herod's murder of his own sons.

Regardless, it is in the realm of possibility that it could have, which makes it easier to consider that if one aspect might be true, who is to say that the rest of it is not? With that in mind, let us delve into the traditional Christmas narrative as presented by the Gospels. And let us start with that account of the atrocity committed by King Herod. If King Herod did indeed do such a terrible thing, this action, while certainly abominable, he would have had a fairly clear-cut reason to do so, at least in his mind.

King Herod was a Roman puppet whose power could have been squashed at any time at Rome's whim. He was only allowed to rule over his people because the Roman emperor allowed him to do so. As the Romans conquered much of the ancient world, they were clever enough to realize that it would be difficult for them to continuously rule over the vast tracts of land they had seized without local allies on the ground. As such, they began a pattern of installing friendly client kings to rule over far-flung territories. And at the time of the birth of Christ, this was very much the case with the region we know as Israel/Palestine.

Rome had given King Herod authority, but at the end of the day, he was seen as Rome's crony. In the eyes of Rome, his number one job was to keep the status quo. The Romans, who were experiencing the Pax Romana or "Roman Peace," liked to keep their dominion as orderly as possible. King Herod was tasked with making sure that his corner of the empire remained peaceful and that no revolts, uprisings, or any other form of obnoxious turmoil came to the attention of his Roman taskmasters.

If Herod failed in this duty, he could be easily dismissed (and possibly killed) by his Roman benefactors. It was, therefore, in Herod's best interest to nip any potential challenge to his (and ultimately Rome's) rule in the bud. And according to the traditional Christmas story, this was what the wily and ruthless Herod was attempting to do during the "slaughter of the innocents." The wise men prophesied to him that a king had been born in Bethlehem. Herod professed interest in seeing this king, but in reality, Herod wanted to kill the newborn king.

The wise men *wised up* to this fact. They realized Herod's true intentions (although the Gospels say an angel warned them) and managed to slip away from Herod without giving him any further information about where Jesus would be born. Infuriated, Herod decided to kill all the kids in Bethlehem who just so happened to be under the age of two in the hopes he would ensnare the newborn Jesus Christ. However, Jesus' earthly father, Joseph, was warned in a dream to gather his family and flee to Egypt.

As the Bible explains, "An angel of the Lord appeared to Joseph in a dream, and said to him, 'Rise up, take the child and his mother and escape with them to Egypt, and stay there until I tell you; for Herod is going to search for the child to do away with him'" (Matthew 2:13-15). As such, they managed to just barely escape the trap that was being set for them.

According to the Gospels, countless other families were not so lucky, and the wails of devastated mothers could be heard all over Israel. Jesus' family made their way to Egypt, where they found refuge for some time. According to the Gospels, they only returned when an angel again visited them and informed them that King Herod had perished.

The death of King Herod is yet another feature of the Christmas story that was mentioned by the historian Josephus. The Gospels tell us that he stepped out in shining garments to speak to a crowd, only to be struck down dead. The Gospels' reasoning behind his death is a bit vague. The Jewish historian Josephus goes into further detail. Herod apparently had been suffering from a wide variety of terrible illnesses and was even plagued with open, infected sores that one might expect from someone suffering from leprosy.

The issue with Herod's death is when he died. Some historians dismiss the stories of Herod the Great in the Bible because they believe he died in 4 BCE, which is before the traditionally accepted date of Jesus' birth. However, biblical scholars do believe that Herod was alive when Jesus was born and think that Jesus might have been born earlier than 1 BCE. Today, it is believed that Jesus was born anywhere between 6 and 4 BCE.

At any rate, after Christ's return to Israel proper, we are not given any other details about Christ's upbringing, save for a mention of a precocious Jesus teaching in the temple. The narrative jumps forward to the start of his earthly ministry. Jesus is believed to have been in his early thirties at the start of his ministry. He lived during a period of great tension between the people of Israel and the Roman authorities.

The Jewish leaders were trying their best to keep the status quo and prevent the wrath of Rome from coming down on them, but the situation was becoming increasingly precarious. The average citizen was crying out in agony under the yoke of Roman oppression and the perceived powerlessness of their own local leaders. There were indeed many looking for what they called the "Messiah," the one who would make all things right once again.

Rather than seeing the Messiah as a harbinger of a new faith, for most Jews, the Messiah was someone who would finally topple Roman authority and bring about a new kingdom of Jerusalem. Jesus himself often spoke of the "coming kingdom." He talked about the "Kingdom of Heaven" being at hand. The Lord's Prayer even invokes the imagery of a kingdom when it states, "Thy Kingdom come, Thy will be done, On Earth as it is in Heaven."

But Christ's conception of the coming kingdom differed from what most of his contemporaries envisioned. Christ was speaking of a "heavenly kingdom" coming down to Earth. He is speaking of heaven as a perfect place of love, justice, and peace and praying that this heavenly kingdom will be brought down to Earth so that Earth will be like heaven.

Jesus' view is much more idealistic than what most of his contemporaries' views would have been. Nevertheless, just as was the case when Jesus was born, with wise men hailing him as the newborn king, the notion that Jesus was speaking of a coming kingdom was used by his opponents to suggest that he was attempting to go against the status quo. They accused him of wanting to topple the current earthly kingdom and install himself as king.

After Jesus got on the bad side of local religious leaders who did not like his preaching, they used these accusations to have him killed. The religious establishment of the time did not take a liking to Jesus for many reasons. To the more pragmatic-minded who wished to maintain the status quo, Jesus was perceived as a great disrupter. His claims of being the Messiah and his statements about the kingdom of heaven being at hand were too disruptive for those who wanted everything to continue as normal.

Although people today tend to view Jesus as a man who inspired others, many back then disliked the attention that Jesus was bringing to the region due to his preaching and miracle. Their window of opportunity to shut down this movement arrived when one of Jesus' disciples betrayed him.

Christ's betrayer, Judas Iscariot, is a complicated figure. Judas did not betray Jesus because he was worried about him disrupting the old order. According to some scholars, Judas was becoming increasingly frustrated with Jesus because he wanted Jesus to take more action and be more disruptive. Judas misunderstood Christ's message and was hoping that he would use his power and influence to overthrow the Roman occupation of the Levant. Since Judas had witnessed Christ's miracles, one could also speculate that Judas believed that Jesus had supernatural powers and would use them to strike any Roman dead who approached.

And considering Judas' actions, it does not seem that his goal was to have Jesus crucified. It seems that he was actually trying to provoke a response from Christ. Judas wanted to be the catalyst that pushed Christ to action (or at least the action that Judas desired from him). It was only when Jesus did not strike down his opponents with fire from heaven, instead allowing himself to be taken prisoner and sent to the cross, that Judas despaired over his actions.

It did not turn out as he had planned. An entirely distraught Judas begged for the religious authorities to release Jesus. As scripture tells us, the religious authorities refused, prompting Judas to throw the thirty pieces of silver they gave him for committing the betrayal at their feet. Judas then went outside and hung himself, unable to live with the knowledge of what he had done.

Jesus was billed as an incorrigible rabble-rouser and disrupter. The religious authorities knew that anyone who was deemed subversive to Rome could be executed. As such, they took Jesus to Pontius Pilate, the governor of the Roman province of Judaea, and charged that he was a revolutionary attempting to take down the Roman Empire. However, it seems Pilate took one look at Jesus and pegged him as more of a philosopher than a political revolutionary. He viewed Christ as a mystic and a dreamer and wished to "wash his hands" of the whole matter.

However, the biblical narrative tells us that no matter what Pilate tried to do to get Jesus released, the local leaders clamored even more vigorously that he be put to death. Finally, they threatened to go above the governor's head. Pilate could not stomach this, so he finally caved into their demands and had Jesus crucified. There are many sources that diverge at this point, but most historians believe that Jesus Christ was crucified.

The greatest divergence of all is over what happened next. For a critic, it is the most important point of contention, and for a Christian, it is the hallmark of their faith. It is said that three days after Jesus was crucified on the cross, he was physically resurrected and rose from the dead. All of the Gospels bear this out, although there are some fairly substantial differences as it pertains to certain details of how it all went down.

For example, the Gospels do not agree on who went to the tomb to discover Christ had been resurrected. Most of the accounts speak of one or two angels greeting them in the tomb and informing them of the risen Christ. Another account insists that Mary Magdalene was in the tomb weeping because she found it empty and believed the body had been taken. She then observed a man whom she thought was the gardener and asked him where the body of Jesus was. The man revealed that he was none other than Jesus Christ.

In one of the most touching scenes from the Bible, Jesus calls Mary by name, and she recognizes him. She cries out of pure joy. But according to the scripture, when she tries to hug Jesus, he warns her not to do so because he has not yet "ascended to the Father."

As the full scripture of John 20:15-17 reads, "He asked her, 'Woman, why are you crying? Who is it you are looking for?' Thinking he was the gardener, she said, "Sir, if you have carried him away, tell me where you have put him, and I will get him.' Jesus said to her, 'Mary.' She turned toward him and cried out in Aramaic, 'Rabboni!' [which means Teacher]. Jesus said, 'Do not hold on to me, for I have not yet ascended to the Father. Go instead to my brothers and tell them, "I am ascending to my Father and your Father, to my God and your God."'"

This statement is important for Christians because the traditional Christian belief is that everyone will be physically resurrected in the end, just like Christ. Believers will also be transformed into "glorified bodies." It is difficult to quantify when this glorification process happened with Christ because shortly after the empty tomb was found, all of the Gospels contend that he appeared on multiple occasions over the next forty days.

On these occasions, Jesus sat down, talked, and even ate with the disciples. And in another dramatic sequence, when his former disciple Thomas expressed doubt, saying that he would only believe if he could put his hands in the holes in Christ's wrist, Jesus appeared directly to him and allowed him to do just that. So, even though Christ warned Mary in the tomb not to touch him because he hadn't been glorified yet, by the time he ran into Thomas, the process was apparently complete since he allowed Thomas to touch his wounds.

According to scripture, after the forty-day period was up, Jesus literally ascended into heaven. During the event known as the "Ascension," the Bible speaks of Christ giving one last sermon to a large crowd before he began floating up into the air. Those down on the ground are said to have strained their eyes to watch the resurrected Christ ascend until their eyes could no longer perceive him.

While they were straining to get one last glimpse of Christ as he ascended higher and higher, they were greeted by a couple of angels on the ground who told them not to worry and that Christ would return one day. Today, many Christians take a more symbolic view of the scripture, especially the more supernatural elements like his ascension and his many miracles. However, we must remember that for the early Christians—and until fairly recently and even today—the faithful read these portrayals as literal accounts.

In other words, it was not perceived as an allegory at all. The Bible said Christ was crucified, he was physically resurrected, and he floated up into the air until he was out of sight. And this is what Christians believed. For them, there was no symbolism. There was Jesus, there was the cross, there was a physical resurrection, and then a risen Christ—end of story.

Chapter 2: The Bible: Meet the Authors

There are some Christian faithful who might take umbrage at even mentioning the "authors" of the Bible. It might seem sacrilegious to them to attempt to dissect and name those who wrote certain verses since they consider it all to be "divinely inspired" or, as it is often said, the literal "Word of God." But those who know the Bible have to admit that it was indeed written by actual people.

One could certainly argue that these authors were tools of God and that they were directed to write what was in God's will, but the authors existed and wrote the passages all the same (although historians now contend that the books may have been written or supplemented by followers of a certain disciple).

It is fairly well known among biblical scholars that Moses was most likely the author of the first five books of the Bible. In Judaism, the first five Mosaic books are called the Torah. This collection includes two of the most powerful books of the Old Testament: Genesis and Exodus.

Exodus deals with how the "children of Israel" were led out of bondage in Egypt. Moses is the central character in this story, as he has the lead role. Most of it is considered to be firsthand accounts, likely all witnessed by Moses himself. For Genesis, Moses had to cast his mind back in time to the beginning of creation.

It is perhaps the notion that Moses was writing the creation story long after it happened that might bother some Christians. Many Jews and Christians believe God dictated the biblical accounts to Moses. But if one wants to stay firmly on the ground or does not believe in Christianity or Judaism, there is a simple explanation for the first five books of the Bible: Moses was not writing eyewitness accounts but was chronicling stories that already existed.

Prior to Moses writing anything down, there was an oral history of what was said to have happened. Whether you believe this oral history passed down all the way from Adam and Eve is up to you.

Many ancient cultures had oral histories that were passed down from generation to generation. This situation changed for the Hebrew people when Moses came along, collected the narratives, and decided to write them all down. Most people believe this is how the Book of Genesis came about, although there are some who contend Moses did not write down anything (there is no firm proof one way or the other). No author was listed, and no author will likely ever be found because society back then didn't consider that important. However, most biblical scholars believe Moses wrote it and that he simply chronicled oral testimonies that had been passed down long before he was even born.

Such a thing becomes easily understandable when one considers the fact that the New Testament accounts of the risen Christ were likely written several years, if not decades, after the fact. Thus, the first accounts of what happened must have been orally transmitted. In other words, one person told another of the astonishing things to which they had borne witness.

The Gospels of Mark, Matthew, Luke, and John are all believed to have been written long after the events they described. There are some who believe that the Book of Mark, which is believed to be the text written closest to the events it describes, may have been written from a previous, older source that has been lost. This could very well be the case, but as of this writing, we do not know this for sure.

So, it is generally accepted that the Gospels were all written at least twenty years after the events they described. We don't know the exact process, but it could be that the authors went around speaking with witnesses who were still alive. It would be like someone in 2023 speaking with survivors of the terrorist attack in New York that took place on September 11th, 2001. The year 2023 is fairly far removed from the year 2001, but it is not that far removed.

And if someone gathered up enough 9/11 survivors with good memories, it is likely that they would have a fairly large amount of source material to use for their book. The same could be said for the authors of the Gospels. And when we say authors of the Gospels, we have to keep in mind that there have long been arguments that the appellations given to these works were primarily pseudonyms. Matthew, Mark, and even Luke have been called into question.

The only book that most scholars consider to be written by the named author is the Gospel of John. But having said that, there is still plenty of room for debate on this issue.

First, let us take a look at the oldest written Gospel, the one that is closest on the timeline to the actual events: the Gospel of Mark. The Gospel of Mark is believed to have been written around 50 CE (so roughly twenty years after the fact).

It has long been believed that Mark was actually an early church figure named John Mark, who was St. Peter's interpreter. He interpreted Peter's words in the early years of the church as the Gospels (or at least the oral transmission of them) were being spread. Since Peter is widely believed to have been illiterate, it is believed that John Mark might have served as a scribe for Peter as well. He has sometimes even been credited as being the one who penned Peter's words in the epistles of 1st and 2nd Peter.

If the Book of Mark was indeed written by a person with such a close relationship to the Apostle Peter, it would greatly bolster the veracity of the accounts. It could be assumed that much of what was written in the Gospel of Mark came straight from the mouth of a chief eyewitness: Apostle Peter. This lends great veracity to the New Testament since this would be about as close of a reference as one could hope to get as it pertained to writing the Gospel since Jesus was unavailable.

Even if it was written down many years later, with John Mark interviewing an elder Peter who was nearing the end of his life, it would still serve as an excellent primary text. Time may have altered some recollections, such as how many angels were in the tomb, but whatever words Mark took from Peter likely was a fairly accurate portrayal of the main events of Christ's ministry. The notion that

Mark used eyewitness testimony may even be alluded to in the next oldest Gospel: the Gospel of Luke.

Luke 1:2 mentions a certain "minister" who gathered up the testimonies of eyewitnesses and other ministers. It is believed that the Gospel of Luke was written roughly ten years after the Gospel of Mark, dating back to around 60 CE, although some believe it took until 80 or 90 since this Gospel was likely a combination of several authors. Luke was largely written as a companion piece to the other book attributed to Luke, the Book of Acts. The Book of Acts is a dynamic work and continues the biblical narrative directly after Christ's ascension.

The Book of Acts describes the early church's struggles and how early church leaders came together. Peter and James played a key role in the Jerusalem church and faced much persecution. Some of this persecution came from the future Apostle Paul. Prior to Paul's conversion to Christianity, he was a zealous Pharisee (a member of a strict Jewish sect) and known as "Saul of Tarsus." The Book of Acts describes how Saul was determined to crush the Christian sect since he sincerely believed they were all a bunch of heretics.

Saul arrested Christians and even oversaw their execution. Such a thing was vividly portrayed in the account of how Stephen was stoned to death after preaching the gospel. Saul was a witness to this killing, and he would come to liken himself to a murderer in his epistles. However, Saul was converted after a mysterious instance occurred to him while traveling the road to Damascus.

The Book of Acts tells us that Christ appeared to Saul and asked him a simple question. "Saul, Saul, why do you persecute me?" Jesus was standing in as the persecuted church, but Saul initially had no idea who he was dealing with and asked the figure, "Who are you?" It was then that Jesus is said to have answered, "I am Jesus, whom you are persecuting."

Saul was then said to have been struck with blindness due to an intense blast of light. He would be healed by one of the Christians at a local church in Damascus, which he had been traveling to in the first place, although his intentions were not good. After his healing, Saul became fully dedicated to the cause of Christianity. It is not known for sure what happened out there on the road to Damascus, but by all accounts, the transformation was incredible.

Ready to embrace a complete change of character, Saul insisted he be called Paul. He went from being one of the most zealous persecutors of the faith to one of the most zealous promoters of the faith. In fact, Paul would give his life for the cause. Although it is not specifically mentioned in the scripture, it is widely believed that he perished in the Neronian persecution of the church, which occurred in 67 CE.

Nero instigated the persecution after a terrible fire burned Rome. Nero blamed the Christians, no doubt citing the fact that many apocalyptic Christian preachers were known for their fire and brimstone sermons about the impending end of the age. So, the idea went that some renegade Christians might have attempted to kickstart the apocalypse by setting Rome on fire!

To this day, no one really knows what happened, but Nero's efforts to scapegoat the Christians ultimately backfired, and he would be blamed. Nero would go down in history as the guy who "fiddled while Rome burned," although this likely never occurred. Even so, before it was all said and done, many Christians, including Apostles Paul and Peter, would be killed in this Roman crackdown on Christians.

Since this event is widely known to have occurred around 67 CE, it is believed that the Book of Acts (which does not specifically mention Paul's or Peter's death) was written a few years prior to this. So, Mark is believed to have been written in the 50s, Luke in the 60s, and the Book of Acts a short time later.

But what about the Book of Matthew? Early church leaders actually thought the Book of Matthew was written first, which explains why it is placed as the first book of the New Testament. Early church fathers thought the Book of Matthew was written around 40 CE. If so, it would have been a fairly fresh account since it would have been compiled just a few years after the events it describes. But this goes against the general consensus of biblical scholars today.

Today, it is widely believed that the Gospel of Matthew must have been written around 80 CE, if not later. Matthew had long been thought to have been compiled by the tax collector Matthew, who was mentioned in the Gospel. In the Book of Matthew, we get a full account of the tax collector whom Jesus—to the chagrin of many of his other followers—had befriended.

Interestingly, Jesus calling a tax collector to the ministry is mentioned in Mark and Luke, except in these two Gospels, he is not referred to as Matthew but rather "Levi." There is a wide range of plausible explanations for this. First of all, Levi is a traditional tribal group within Israel. Also, Levi could have been this person's Hebrew name, with Matthew being his Hellenized Greek name. There is also the chance that Jesus renamed Levi the tax collector as Matthew when he joined the ministry.

There is a precedence for this. Such a thing would have been similar to Jesus declaring that Simon Bar-Jonah (Apostle Peter) was "Petros" or the "rock" on which he would build his church. The Greek word for rock is *petros*, which would ultimately be rendered in subsequent translations as "Peter."

At any rate, if we entertain the notion that Matthew or Levi, the tax collector and a contemporary of Christ, wrote down this particular Gospel, it would be a very important account since it would have been written by someone who was there on the ground when much of it happened.

However, most scholars today date the Book of Matthew to around 80 CE. Matthew would have been an elderly man at the time this account was written. People simply did not live as long as they do now, which casts doubt on the theory that Matthew wrote the account. While it is true that the average person may have perished at fifty rather than seventy or eighty, there were always a few outliers. Such instances may have been rare, but they did occur. So, it would not be out of the realm of reason that Matthew just so happened to be among those rare few.

After all, it is widely believed that the author of the Book of John, John the Revelator, lived to a fairly old age. Speaking of John, the Gospel of John perhaps has the most widely agreed-upon precepts. Both the early church and modern scholars believe that the book is likely the last of the Gospels to have been written.

It is evident that the church believed as much due to the simple fact that the Book of John was placed last. Modern-day scholars and historians have plenty of reasons for believing that the Book of John was the last and final Gospel to be included. The Gospel itself has some clues to its finality.

As John 21:24-25 relates, "This is the disciple who is testifying to these things and has written them, and we know that his testimony is true; but there are also many other things that Jesus did; if all of them were written down, I suppose that the world itself would not contain the books that would be written."

Yes, lending credence to the notion that John had the last word as it pertains to the Gospels, this statement sounds almost like someone was making a "case closed" definitive argument. John is acknowledging here that there are many things that Jesus might have done that were not included in the testimony simply due to the fact that they were too numerous to tell.

But the question remains, who is the author? Was it really the Apostle John? Or was it someone else?

As early as 180 CE, an early church father by the name of Irenaeus, a known authority on matters of scripture, declared that this particular Gospel was written by the Apostle John. According to Irenaeus, "John, the disciple of the Lord, who also had leaned upon His breast, did himself publish a Gospel during his residence at Ephesus in Asia."

If we do assume that John was the writer, it must be acknowledged that the Gospel of John has some striking differences compared to the previous Gospels. The Gospel of John is much more oriented toward the Greek concept of the divine. After all, the Greek philosopher Plato spoke of there being a supreme all-powerful force of good known as the "Logos."

Plato believed that it was from the Logos that all things originated, and yet the Logos—this ultimate force—was still connected to all of the creations that had emanated from it. But what does all this have to do with the Gospel of John? Plenty! The Book of John starts off by stating, "In the beginning was the Word." Well, actually, in the original Greek, John wrote, "In the beginning was the Logos."

And that makes all the difference in the world. John was intentionally invoking the Greek concept of the Logos and associating it with Jesus. Here is the full passage, with "Logos" replacing "Word." "In the beginning was the Logos, and the Logos was with God, and the Logos was God. Through him all things were made; without him nothing was made that has been made. The Logos became flesh and made his dwelling among us. We have seen his glory, the glory of the one and only Son, who came from the Father, full of grace and truth."

These complicated concepts find their way into scripture in an almost subliminal fashion, but the Greek-speaking world most certainly would have picked up on the mention of "Logos." John was saying that Jesus was the Logos and that the Logos had been made flesh to "dwell" on Earth. The Greeks thought that the "divine mind" of the Logos periodically sent out its divine thoughts in what was known as "emanations," which manifested into actual beings.

Interestingly enough, these Platonist notions are quite similar to beliefs in Hinduism. Many misunderstand the Hindu faith as being polytheistic, but this is not the case. While it is true that Hindus have a wide variety of god-like figures, Hindus, like the Greeks, believe that everything ultimately came from one eternal god. Whether it's Lord Vishnu, a human being, a tree, or your cat Fluffy, everything ultimately emanates from one divine source. The Hindus called this divine source the "Brahman," whereas the Greeks called it the "Logos."

The fact that a Gospel writer would try to reconcile Greek philosophy with Christian theology was not a unique phenomenon in the 1ˢᵗ century. There was quite a bit of cross-pollination between the two. This was also the case with Christianity's predecessor Judaism, as it was seen in the efforts of intellectuals like the Jewish thinker Philo.

Philo did something quite similar to what John did, except he actually stated that Moses was the Logos. One could argue that Philo's assertion is a bit harder to comprehend since we have scenes of Moses standing before the burning bush as a manifestation of the eternal God, who insists that he is "I AM." In other words, he is the original, all-encompassing reality. He is the Logos.

Did Philo think that the burning bush and Moses were both manifestations of the Logos at the same time and that their dialogue was merely an illusion of two beings who were one and the same but being made to appear separate? It would be similar to how many Christians have notions that God the Father, God the Son, and the Holy Spirit are three parts of the same person. Yes, this sort of theological discourse can get rather complicated.

At any rate, the Gospel of John has the same main narrative as the other Gospels, but it does not go into as much detail. It seems that some of these extra details that were omitted were instead replaced with much more lengthy discourses on philosophical or spiritual beliefs. And then, after it's all said and done, the author seems to have acknowledged this omission. In fact, the author basically apologizes for it by rationalizing that there just was not enough room to include everything. (All the world could not hold it!)

As for the other authors of the Christian scriptures, we would be quite remiss if we did not mention Apostle Paul. To this day, it's still frequently argued over whether or not Paul even realized that his epistles would be included in the actual Christian canon. It must be remembered that epistles were simply letters. Paul's writings were letters that he had penned to local churches or believers in which he expounded upon his beliefs and issued words of encouragement.

Paul was a prolific and profound writer, although the authorship of some of his letters is disputed. Despite this, much of his tremendous insight, although ostensibly directed at just one particular church, such as the "Church of the Corinthians," the "Church of the Galatians," or the "Church of the Romans," were so eloquent and rich that they can quite easily be applied to all believers in general. People today still draw great inspiration from Paul's works.

But having said that, we cannot forget that Paul was writing letters to specific churches and specific people. The fact that he ended up in the Bible at all would be akin to someone writing a book on business management and then finding some really good e-mails Steve Jobs wrote to Steve Wozniak and just slapping them in the book.

That is not to take away from how moving and inspirational Paul's words are, but the fact that he wrote letters rather than Gospels makes it unclear whether he ever intended for his writing to be included in the canon.

Having said that, Paul's writings have often caused a bit of dissension in the church. There have always been those who absolutely swore by them, but there have also been those who warned against them.

Even Apostle Peter seemed somewhat conflicted. Peter simultaneously praised Paul but also issued a kind of cryptic warning about his teachings. In one of Peter's epistles, we find Peter saying, "And count the patience of our Lord as salvation, just as our beloved brother Paul also wrote to you according to the wisdom given him, as he does in all his letters when he speaks in them of these matters.

There are some things in them that are hard to understand, which the ignorant and unstable twist to their own destruction, as they do the other scriptures" (2nd Peter 3:15-16).

Peter does not say that Paul is wrong, but he warns that he speaks about complex theological beliefs that many who are "ignorant" get mixed up and misunderstand what he is talking about. Interestingly enough, later Christian writers of the 2nd century would blame Paul for inspiring the Christian Gnostics.

The Gnostics denied the physical resurrection and further insisted that all physical reality was evil and that the end goal was to be released and become a spirit. And the Gnostics indeed favored Paul, counting him as a fellow Gnostic and seeing him as a great inspiration. This was apparently because they enjoyed the fact that Paul seemed to castigate the flesh just like they wished to do. Paul stated, "Flesh and blood will not inherit the kingdom of God."

This statement, which was written in one of Paul's epistles, seems to endorse the later Gnostic view that flesh and blood are inherently evil. But while seeming to bolster the Gnostics, the troubling verse is completely at odds with all other aspects of the Christian faith. The cornerstone of Christianity is the physical resurrection of Jesus. And during the ascension, people apparently stood and watched as Christ floated up into the skies.

Furthermore, original Christian doctrine attests that all (believers and non-believers) will be physically resurrected in the end. Some would be resurrected to bliss, while others would be resurrected to face judgment. So, one really has to wonder where did Apostle Paul get the idea that "flesh and blood will not inherit the kingdom of God?"

According to the rest of the Bible, when New Jerusalem comes to Earth and the physically resurrected Jesus returns, the saints will also be physically resurrected. All of the erstwhile believers will take part in a very real kingdom of God. It will be just like the Lord's Prayer: "on Earth as it is in Heaven."

Considering all of this, it is quite clear that whatever Paul's intentions were, his words in this particular passage—as Peter warned might happen—cause plenty of confusion, even today. Despite this one random statement about flesh and blood not inheriting the kingdom of God, Paul himself seems to have thoroughly believed in the physical resurrection.

Paul clarified this belief in a profound way in his famous letter to the Church of Corinth by stating, "If there is no resurrection of the dead, then not even Christ has been raised. And if Christ has not been raised, our preaching is useless, and so is your faith. More than that, we are then found to be false witnesses about God, for we have testified about God that he raised Christ from the dead. But he did not raise him if in fact the dead are not raised" (1st Corinthians 15:13-15).

If these words to the Corinthians came after his declaration that "flesh and blood do not inherit the kingdom of God," one would think he was doing a bit of damage control. Perhaps some of the "ignorant" new believers that Peter spoke of took his words and ran with them. Maybe they went around shouting from the roofs, "Paul said flesh and blood do not inherit the kingdom of God; therefore, there is no resurrection!"

But this was not the case at all since these words, which seemingly clarify the physical resurrection, come from the same exact epistle in which Paul crafted the words "flesh and blood do not inherit the kingdom of God." In fact, Paul made this clarification *before* he uttered those infamous words. Paul had been doing everything he could to insist that the physical resurrection of the dead was indeed what Christians should be looking forward to.

Paul then goes on to state, "For if the dead are not raised, then Christ has not been raised either. And if Christ has not been raised, your faith is futile; you are still in your sins. Then those also who have fallen asleep in Christ are lost. If we have hoped in Christ only in this life, we are of all people most to be pitied. But Christ has indeed been raised from the dead, the first fruits of those who have fallen asleep. For since death came through a man, the resurrection of the dead comes also through a man. For as in Adam all die, so in Christ all will be made alive" (1st Corinthians 16:16-22).

Yet as Paul continues his long, complex theological musings, toward the end of this very same epistle, he makes the statement, "I declare to you, brothers and sisters, that flesh and blood cannot inherit the kingdom of God, nor does the perishable inherit the imperishable" (1st Corinthians 15:50).

So, did Paul speak in riddles? As Peter warned, it could just be that some of his sayings are hard to understand at times. If Paul was just using "flesh and blood" as a euphemism for "sinfulness," his words make sense. There are many to this day who might equate "sin" with "fleshly" behavior. Thus, it is possible Paul saying "flesh and blood" or "sinful behavior" will not allow one access to the kingdom of God.

Such a statement would have lined up with previous teachings without any problems. But if this was simply Paul's shorthand at work, only those who knew him well enough to understand his lingo would have fully grasped what he meant. Thus, it is important to consider his audience. He was speaking directly to the congregation at Corinth. Paul had received word they were engaging in inappropriate behavior, so he was correcting them. This could very well be why he warned them to cease and desist their "fleshly" works since it would do nothing to promote their growth as Christians.

Moving on from Paul as a biblical author, the only other acknowledged authors who remain are two brothers of Jesus—James and Jude. Now when we say the word "brothers," we have to be careful because the mention of Jesus having flesh and blood relations often causes some contention among Christians. Through the Christian lens, Jesus was born of his mother, Mary, through the agency of God, making him the "son of God."

Even if you believe in the immaculate conception, there is no denying that Mary and her husband, Joseph, had children together after Jesus was born. So, even if you believe that Jesus was the son of God and Mary, her subsequent children would be Jesus' half-siblings. Thus, the New Testament authors James and Jude were the half-brothers of Jesus, depending on your view of the immaculate conception.

When one thinks about it, it really is quite remarkable that Jesus' two brothers—especially James—did not write more than they did. James has two epistles attributed to him, and the words of Jude are nothing more than a footnote right before the epic final book of the Bible: the Book of Revelation. James' briefness is especially surprising since, after the resurrection, he became a major leader of the Jerusalem church.

James has an interesting backstory. It is said that he initially did not believe his brother's claims. The incontrovertible proof of the resurrected Christ appearing to James made him change his mind. From that point on, James apparently became a zealous promoter of the faith and would lead the Church of Jerusalem for many years. James was ultimately martyred for his faith, but two epistles, 1ˢᵗ and 2ⁿᵈ James, are attributed to him.

Jude's contribution was very minimal but provides us with one of the most interesting passages in the Bible. Jude actually references the once-lost Book of Enoch, speaking of how the fallen angels had come to Earth and interbred with human women, creating half-angel, half-human creatures called the Nephilim.

Jude alludes states, "And the angels who did not keep their positions of authority but abandoned their proper dwelling—these he has kept in darkness, bound with everlasting chains for judgment on the great day" (Jude 1: 6). Jude also strangely warns against "slandering celestial beings." He goes on to state, "In the very same way, on the strength of their dreams these ungodly people pollute their own bodies, reject authority and heap abuse on celestial beings. But even the archangel Michael, when he was disputing with the devil about the body of Moses, did not himself dare to condemn him for slander but said, 'The Lord rebuke you!' Yet these people slander whatever they do not understand, and the very things they do understand by instinct—as irrational animals do—will destroy them" (Jude 1: 8-10).

It is interesting to note the sense of familiarity with which Jude refers to "celestial beings," considering that the Gospels speak of how angels repeatedly visited both of his parents during the Christmas story. Could he be speaking from some of his own personal experiences with these celestial beings? If you believe the family was visited by angels during the Christmas story, it is not much of a leap to imagine that these visitations might have continued as Jesus, James, and Jude grew up under Mary and Joseph's roof.

At any rate, even though the Book of Enoch was not included in the official canon, Jude goes on to reference it once again as a means of describing how he viewed the current state of the church. Jude declares, "Enoch, the seventh from Adam, prophesied about them: 'See, the Lord is coming with thousands upon thousands of his holy ones to judge everyone, and to convict all of them of all the ungodly acts they have committed in their ungodliness, and of all their defiant words ungodly sinners have spoken against him.' These people are grumblers and faultfinders; they follow their own evil desires; they boast about themselves and flatter others for their own advantage" (Jude 1: 14-16).

Jude's message is most certainly an intense one. He again alludes to the celestial host, stating that "the Lord is coming with thousands upon thousands of his holy ones to judge everyone." He then ends his missive with an exclamation by enjoining believers to "be merciful to those who doubt; save others by snatching them from the fire; to others show mercy, mixed with fear—hating even the clothing stained by corrupted flesh."

This seems like a final closing statement. And if the Book of Revelation was not included in the Bible, one could almost envision these being the definitive words of the scripture before closing the book. Interestingly enough, there were some who wanted to take out the Book of Revelation. Martin Luther famously wished to remove it from the Protestant canon.

However, Luther had his own reasons, as he felt that the Book of Revelation's mention of casting "Hades" (a temporary place) into the "Lake of Fire" (an apparently eternal final destination) sounded as if it bolstered the Catholic concept of the temporary holding place of purgatory, which he was against at the time.

Speaking of the Book of Revelation, it is believed that the same author of the Gospel of John was the author of this prophetic work. When John was sent into exile by the Romans to the island of Patmos, he had several revelatory experiences. John apparently wrote down what he saw, rendering a long narrative of prophetic imagery. There is quite a bit of argument to this day over how much of the Book of Revelation is literal and how much is symbolic.

There are some who would like to take a completely literal stance, but this is rather hard to fathom since at the beginning of the Book of Revelation, the angel who begins John's presentation of revelatory imagery uses the symbolism of "seven lampstands," which the angel itself insists represents the "seven churches" that were present in Asia Minor. Since the angel said as much during the revelation itself, it seems pretty clear that at least some parts of the Book of Revelation were meant to be symbolic. But even so, the question remains, where do you draw the line?

What's symbolic? And what's not? Continuing in this vein, perhaps one of the more perplexing issues is when John bore witness to the "Battle of Armageddon." He apparently saw armies wielding swords and fighting on horseback. This would have been common fare in John's age, but in the modern world, we view Armageddon as being fought by tanks and jet fighters.

For portions of this scripture, symbolism is usually invoked. For example, when John is presented with imagery of "locusts" that bring death to a large portion of humanity, some have theorized that John was actually being shown modern-day Apache attack helicopters, which, to an untrained eye, do resemble locusts. And if John, who had no idea what a helicopter was, saw this great contraption, he likely would have identified it as some great beast he was familiar with, like a locust.

At any rate, John's prophecies have long been argued over in a wide variety of ways. Many argue whether or not these prophecies had already occurred, if all of them were yet to come, or if he had any prophecies in the first place.

At any rate, these were the authors of the scripture, and their influence on Christianity continues to this day.

Chapter 3: Christianity Takes Shape

Although Christianity was founded by Christ, it was built by Christ's followers. And the core of this religious zeal for the purportedly resurrected Jesus can be traced back to the group of people who claimed to have seen him resurrected, from his first alleged appearances at the tomb to his further appearances in homes, on roadsides, and speaking before vast multitudes. According to the scripture, Christ's resurrection set a fire in his followers and caused them to "turn the world upside down" for him.

Whether you believe the resurrection happened or not, one has to concede that early Christians believed in it. And such an event is a good explanation as to why the first Christians became so galvanized to preach the gospel. We see this at work in the attitudes of Christ's closest disciples. Immediately after the crucifixion, they were a depressed and paranoid lot. They stayed indoors and kept their heads low in fear that with Jesus gone, they might be next. The best terms to describe their state of mind might be defeated, dispirited, hunted, and hounded.

Yet, according to the scripture, on that third day, the resurrected Christ appeared before them. Everything changed. Their sadness turned to joy, and their fear turned into certainty that the cause they believed in was right and just. They were so sure of themselves that they barged right into the middle of the temple to declare Christ had been resurrected from the dead, even though they knew they could be arrested and put to death just for saying as much.

Acts 4:7-13 has a very powerful account of this, depicting Peter fearlessly standing up to the temple authorities. It reads, "Then Peter, filled with the Holy Spirit, said to them: 'Rulers and elders of the people! If we are being called to account today for an act of kindness shown to a man who was lame and are being asked how he was healed, then know this, you and all people of Israel: It is by the name of Jesus Christ of Nazareth, whom you crucified but whom God raised from the dead, that this man stands before you healed. Jesus is the stone you builders rejected, which has become the cornerstone. Salvation is found in no one else, for there is no other name under heaven given to mankind by which we must be saved.'"

Bold words like this could have brought about immediate death. When Peter spoke them, he was said to have miraculously healed a lame man by praying in the name of Jesus. And when questioned about it, rather than denying Christ, as Peter had done prior to the resurrection, he boldly proclaimed his belief in Christ. He stood up to those in charge and declared that he would never stop proclaiming Christ and basically dared them to do their worst.

One has to ask, why would he be willing to die for a lie? It is hard enough for many people to die for the truth, let alone something someone has made up. The fact that these men and women were willing to die rather than renounce Christ is a strong testament to the fact that—if anything else—they truly believed what they were saying. We can argue that they were delusional, but whatever was going on, they sincerely seemed to believe in the resurrection of Jesus Christ.

At any rate, the purported resurrection served as the catalyst that sent the early church into action. Christ's followers would preach openly in the streets of Jerusalem and then make their way much farther afield. By the 2nd century, Christianity had spread, to some degree, to virtually all of the Roman Empire.

During this period, Christians were periodically tolerated and persecuted by various Roman regimes and Roman citizens. Much of this persecution was often based on simple misunderstandings as to what Christianity was all about. For example, Christians were secretive about their gatherings and often met in graveyards. The Christians likely met there because they could meet there in peace without being bothered.

But for anyone who was not a Christian and happened to see a congregation gathering in a graveyard themselves, it would have been quite a strange sight to behold. Christians were also accused of cannibalism due to a misunderstanding of Communion. This perhaps sounds like nonsense to us today, but consider the words attributed to Christ for the ceremony: "This is my blood, this is my body." For those who did not know the symbolism or what it all meant, it is easy to see why they thought Christians were talking about drinking blood and eating people.

Because of all of these misunderstandings, Christian apologists became prominent. To be clear, a Christian apologist was not someone apologizing for their faith. On the contrary, an apologist was someone who clarified and defended their faith. The word "apologist" comes from the Greek word *apologia*, which literally means "defense." One of the most famous Christian apologists was Justin Martyr, who lived during the 2nd century and wrote long treatises defending Christian beliefs in terms that are fairly familiar to Christian ideology in the modern age.

And by the 4th century, a large chunk of the Roman empire was Christian. In 313 CE, Roman Emperor Constantine issued his famous Edict of Milan, in which he declared Christianity a lawful, tolerated religion. The church, which had once been so persecuted, would become the main religion of the Roman Empire. And shortly after this, what we know today as the Catholic (universal) Church was formed.

However, the Catholic Church claims that its roots go all the way back to Apostle Peter when he became the first bishop of Rome (making him the first pope) shortly before he was martyred. Catholics can point to a long history of stewardship, at least as it pertains to the role of the bishop of Rome (also known as the pope). Pope Linus, a man who was said to have been personally picked by Peter himself to be his successor, took on the mantle after Peter. Linus was also mentioned in one of the letters to Timothy (2nd Timothy 4:21, to be exact). And the line of popes has continued to this very day.

At any rate, after the Christian-friendly Roman Emperor Constantine decided that Christianity should be tolerated, he became determined to use it as a binding, unifying force. But to do this, there had to be a set standard, a universal doctrine that all Christians must abide by. Constantine's sheer ambition to achieve this goal led to one of the most consequential events in Christian history: the Council of Nicaea. Held in 325 CE in the eastern Mediterranean city of Nicaea, church leaders came together to formulate the universal church doctrine that would be known as the Nicene Creed.

This creed was the official professed statement of what Christians proclaimed to believe. It cut through nearly three centuries of confusion, during which time Christians vigorously debated among themselves about everything from Communion to the nature of Christ's divinity.

Those gathered at the Council of Nicaea proclaimed:

"I believe in one God, the Father almighty, maker of Heaven and Earth, of all things visible and invisible. I believe in one Lord Jesus Christ, the Only Begotten Son of God, born of the Father before all ages. God from God, Light from Light, true God from true God, begotten, not made, consubstantial with the Father; through him all things were made. For us men and for our salvation he came down from Heaven, and by the Holy Spirit was incarnate of the Virgin Mary, and became man. For our sake he was crucified under Pontius Pilate, he suffered death and was buried, and rose again on the third day in accordance with the Scriptures. He ascended into Heaven and is seated at the right hand of the Father. He will come again in glory to judge the living and the dead, and his kingdom will have no end. I believe in the Holy Spirit, the Lord, the giver of life, who proceeds from the Father and the Son, who with the Father and the Son is adored and glorified, who has spoken through the prophets. I believe in one, holy Catholic and Apostolic Church. I confess one baptism for the forgiveness of sins, and I look forward to the resurrection of the dead and the life of the world to come. Amen."

Even in this creed, you once again see the word "Catholic" or "universal" being stressed. Constantine's project was a big one, as he wished to unite all Christians in his realm under one banner. Considering the divergence of views that existed prior to the Council of Nicaea, it really is rather incredible that the council was as successful as it was in uniting the factions.

It is said that church leaders from far and wide traveled to Nicaea and vigorously debated their views on scripture before they came up with this universal creed. Just imagine all of these elder statesmen of the church, some still bearing the visible scars of previous persecutions, gathering to hammer these things out together.

Once this "universal" or "Catholic" church was established, it was up to church leaders and subsequent Roman rulers to make sure that it did not fall apart. The institutions that were established were fairly strong.

The Roman Catholic Church has indeed stood the test of time. The Catholic Church survived the fall of the Western Roman Empire, safeguarding not only Christianity but also Roman civic customs and bureaucracy. If one really thinks about it, the structure of the Catholic Church is largely parallel with the structure of the old Roman government.

The pope is essentially an emperor, and his multitude of cardinals in the Vatican serve basically the same role as senators did in the Roman Senate. The Church of Rome was so strong that even after barbarian armies poured into the "Eternal City," the barbarians chose to submit to the pope and become Catholic themselves instead of toppling the institution!

Some of these newcomers had already become Christians prior to Rome's fall. Roman emperors had long recruited warriors from surrounding regions, and many were introduced to the Christian faith while fighting for Rome in this capacity. There were many incentives for them to do so; for instance, it would be in their best interest to better identify with their Roman taskmasters. This early contingent of converts would better aid the conversion of later subsequent waves of pagans.

Shortly after Rome fell in 476 CE, one of the warlords, a Frankish king named Clovis, was convinced to drop his pagan beliefs and become a Christian. Demonstrating how widespread Christianity had become, his own wife, Clotilde, was already a Christian before Clovis changed religions. Clovis had his own problems. He faced constant warfare with the various tribes that had descended upon the western half of the Roman Empire, so he was being pressed in on all sides. Allegedly in the midst of a fierce battle, in which he feared all was lost, he called upon the Christian God for help.

In many ways, it was a repeat of the miraculous sign that former Roman Emperor Constantine the Great was said to have experienced.

Constantine was in the middle of a pitched battle when he supposedly saw a flaming cross in the sky. He took this as a sign to trust in Christ, so he rallied his troops and emerged victorious. In a similar way, Clovis saw what he interpreted as a supernatural victory, although it is not known for sure what he saw.

After this, he apparently submitted to Christianity and to the pope in Rome. Not only that, but he also directed all of his followers to do the same. This would be a continuing trend in western Europe, which allowed the Catholic Church to thrive, despite the fact that the Western Roman Empire was in ruins.

In the meantime, the Eastern Roman Empire, which would become known as the Byzantine Empire, continued to thrive. Constantine founded the Eastern Roman capital of Constantinople on the old site of the Greek city of Byzantium in Asia Minor (modern-day Turkey). The Eastern Roman Empire would continue for quite some time, with its own emperor ruling from Constantinople.

Although the West and the East were politically separated, their tenuous connection through the Catholic Church would remain for the next few centuries. Even so, many differences began to surface. These differences were both of a political and theological nature. For one thing, the Eastern Roman emperors in Constantinople thoroughly expected the pope in Rome to recognize them as the legitimate Roman emperor.

This became an odder and odder prospect. The Byzantines had waged a losing war against the Ostrogoths in Italy, yet any real imperial hold of Rome was fleeting at best. Yet the Byzantine emperor still wanted the pope to recognize him as sovereign, even though the Eastern emperor was not fulfilling his role as the protector of Rome or the pope. Such a relationship was bound to come to ruin.

Despite any claims to the contrary, the popes were increasingly dependent upon friendly kings in the West for military aid rather than the Eastern Roman emperor. For instance, in 754, the Lombards attempted an all-out invasion of Italy. The pope turned to a Frankish (as in French) king in the West for aid.

The so-called "Apostle of Germany," Saint Boniface, had been friendly with King Pepin of the Franks, and this friendship paid off when King Pepin was persuaded to stop the Lombard advance in its tracks. Not only that, but his armies also gifted the sitting pope, Pope

Stephen II, with large tracts of land they had seized in central Italy, which would become known as the Papal States. Ever since the fall of Rome, the popes had long learned to become Machiavellian strategists of the greatest sort, balancing one power on top of another just to keep their heads above water.

But now, the popes turned to the Franks of western Europe. In 799, Pope Leo III was nearly beaten to death in the street. This rather under-protected pope came to the pragmatic realization that his relationship with the Franks should be made binding. So, in 800, Pope Leo III infuriated the Byzantines by crowning King Charlemagne of the Franks as the "Holy Roman Emperor."

Charlemagne would go on to found what would later be known as the "Holy Roman Empire," which consisted of modern-day Germany, most of France, and northern Italy. And until Napoleon toppled it, the Holy Roman Empire would have a long line of emperors who descended from Charlemagne.

At any rate, back in 800 CE, when the pope crowned Charlemagne emperor and made him the temporal "defender of the faith," the Eastern Roman emperor was furious. This was perhaps the first major fissure between Western and Eastern relations, although theological differences were already present. After this sundering of the political relationship between East and West, the theological differences began to fester. These differences would only grow worse until a "Great Schism" ensued.

Chapter 4: The Great Schism (1054 CE)

It occurred seemingly without warning one sunny day in 1054. The pope's personal legate, Cardinal Humbert, was in Constantinople paying a visit to the great Greek monastery, the Hagia Sophia. He was not there to pay respects, though; rather, he was there to inflame sentiments. Upon entering the church, he walked right up to the altar and deposited an official bull of excommunication squarely on it. As the cardinal and his fellow colleagues from Rome filed out of the church, they were followed by a local priest, who, realizing what had happened, began to plead with them to reconsider.

However, the papal legate was entirely unmoved, and the excommunication stood. But as sudden as all this seemed, the tremors beneath this theological earthquake between the Christian East and the Christian West had been going on for quite some time. Some have since tried to argue that the Great Schism of 1054 was similar to a medieval reformation. But it must be said that what happened in 1054 was much more political than it was spiritual.

Even though some fairly minor doctrinal differences were highlighted, the key dispute was over sovereignty and who should have it. The dispute involved four figures vying for various forms of power—the pope of Rome, the Holy Roman emperor, the patriarch of Constantinople, and the Byzantine emperor. Ever since the Latin pope decided to crown the Frankish king, Charlemagne, as emperor, great animosity had been building over the exact order of temporal and spiritual power.

For the Byzantines, the fact that the pope would turn to the West and hail a Western ruler as emperor smacked of betrayal. The Byzantines viewed Charlemagne as an unworthy usurper of the imperial title and the pope's decision to crown him as a terrible error. In the minds of the Byzantines, this act was schismatic.

Fast forward to the 11th century, and the political discord created all those years prior provided the perfect backdrop for exacerbating certain theological tensions. The East, for example, had taken umbrage to the fact that the West had added the phrase "and the Son" to the Nicene Creed. The traditional creed was modified to state that the "Holy Spirit" came not only from the "Father" but also the "Son."

This modification was minor yet major at the same time. Not all Greeks necessarily disagreed with the notion, but it was viewed as an unauthorized adaptation. The real point of contention was the authorization to edit the creed. The East was sick and tired of the West trying to call all the shots. And when it was learned that Greeks in Byzantine enclaves in Italy were being forced to abide by the Latin creed, the patriarch of Constantinople, Michael Cerularius, took action by insisting that Latin Catholics in Constantinople be forced to use the Greek version.

The Latin Catholics refused, and the Greek patriarch retaliated by shutting their churches down. All of this led to the pope sending his legates, who were led by Cardinal Humbert, to Constantinople in 1054 to see if some compromise could be made. The attempt at reconciliation did not go well, so Cardinal Humbert, who claimed to have authority given to him by the pope, dropped the bombshell: the infamous bull of excommunication.

Not to be outdone and true to form, the patriarch then turned around and excommunicated Pope Leo IX. However, the pope had already perished, doing so in April. Word traveled slowly in those days, and unbeknownst to both parties, Pope Leo had passed away while Cardinal Humbert was busy excommunicating the Greek patriarch in his name. If Leo had died, did Humbert have the authority to excommunicate the patriarch? Technically, he did not, but the damage had already been done. The West and the East now viewed each other as heretics.

This was a shocking move, but it would take some time for the direct split of the two main branches of the church to be felt. So, what caused this breach? On the surface, it appears that these two religious leaders were quarreling over minor issues, such as the use of unleavened bread in the Eucharist. And while these issues were important to them, they likely would not have caused a major fallout in the church. Most historians believe the larger issue was about who was calling the shots.

The Western popes wanted to maintain papal supremacy, meaning they wanted to be the top religious leader in charge. But the patriarch of faraway Constantinople disagreed.

The Great Schism would continue to grow and be exacerbated further by political problems. As the Christian West grew stronger politically and militarily, the old Christian East grew weaker. Constantinople was being increasingly threatened by the Turkic tribes of Anatolia (modern-day Turkey).

The Turks had adopted Islam several centuries before, and their warlord leaders had made it, more or less, their goal to topple what remained of the Byzantine Empire. They were quite good at chipping away at this ancient institution, and this threat to the empire's continued stability led the Byzantine emperor to plead with the pope for aid.

Yes, it is indeed ironic that one of the roots of the Great Schism was the fact that the pope had decided to turn away from Constantinople in 800 CE in favor of strong Western rulers, such as Charlemagne. This was done out of the pragmatic reality that the Eastern emperor was no longer able to defend the faith when push came to shove.

Yet, by the end of the 11th century, the Byzantine emperor was not only failing to physically defend the pope, but he was also pleading for the pope to defend him! And his request did not fall on deaf ears. Due to the Byzantine emperor's pleas and reports of Christian pilgrims being harassed in the Holy Land, Pope Urban II launched his famous call for a crusade in that fateful year of 1095.

The Great Schism was in recent memory, so it is likely Urban was hoping to reconcile the church and heal the division. And the subsequent military aid mustered by the West led to the East reconsidering its drift from Rome. Until the fall of Constantinople in 1453, many efforts were made to patch things up. There were even a few declarations that a reunion of the East and West would happen. The most famous of these was, no doubt, the Council of Florence.

This ecumenical council took place between 1431 and 1449. Under great pressure and threat of being overrun by the Ottoman Turks, the Eastern Church grudgingly agreed to the terms of the Council of Florence, with only one Byzantine bishop, Mark of Ephesus, protesting the decision. Mark, who would later be hailed as a saint in the Orthodox Church, wrote a stinging rebuke of the whole exchange.

In 1440, he penned a letter that rejected everything for which the Council of Florence stood. The letter began with the following:

"From Mark, Bishop of the Metropolis of Ephesus—Rejoice in Christ!

To those who have ensnared us in an evil captivity—desiring to lead us away into the Babylon of Latin rites and dogmas—could not, of course, completely accomplish this, seeing immediately that there was little chance of it. In fact, that it was simply impossible."

Mark of Ephesus then went on to note that even after all of the pressure and prodding, the Latin Catholics could only manage a botched compromise of sorts that "stopped somewhere in the middle." Mark rails against the clumsy way that compromises between the Greek and Latin rites were made and deems both approaches to be absolutely worthless. He likened it to resembling the mismatched "centaur" of ancient myth. The centaur was not quite human but not quite animal, and Mark railed against the compromise as being a "false union" that was not quite Latin yet not quite Greek either.

He then went on to state, "But one should examine in what manner they have united with them; for everything that is united to something different is naturally united by means of some middle point between them. And thus they imagined to unite with them by means of some judgment concerning the Holy Spirit, together with expressing the opinion that He has existence also from the Son. But everything else between them is divergent, and there is among them neither any middle point nor anything in common."

Mark highlighted the folly of making compromises over which side of the debate was right. In his mind, either the Latins were right and the Greeks were wrong, or the Greeks were right and the Latins were wrong! For him, compromising over such crucial aspects of religious doctrine to claim that the East and the West were united, resolving the Great Schism in the process, was utterly absurd.

Mark of Ephesus summed up his thoughts by stating, "If, then, the Latins do not at all depart from the correct Faith, we have evidently cut them off unjustly. But if they have thoroughly departed [from the Faith]—and that in connection with the theology of the Holy Spirit, blasphemy against whom is the greatest of all perils—then it is clear that they are heretics, and we have cut them off as heretics."

Obviously, St. Mark of Ephesus took a hardline view of the Orthodox brethren of old, saying that it was the Catholics of the Latin West who were the heretics and not the Greek Christians of the Orthodox East! Sentiments like this, of course, had led to the infamous excommunications in 1054. With both theological barrels firing, Mark of Ephesus then entirely unloads on his theological opponents, declaring:

"If the Latin dogma is true that the Holy Spirit proceeds also from the Son, then ours is false that states that the Holy Spirit proceeds from the Father—and this is precisely the reason for which we separated from them. And if ours is true, then without a doubt, theirs is false. What kind of middle ground can there be between two such judgments? There can be none, unless it were some kind of judgment suitable to both the one and the other, like a boot that fits both feet. And will this unite us?"

For Mark of Ephesus, the notion that such incompatible views could be united together was patently absurd, about as absurd as the centaurs described in ancient Greek myths. Yet, on the official level, the union went forward. The East came to terms with the Latin version of the Nicene Creed and the nature of papal authority. In return, the Byzantine emperor hoped the pope would call another crusade that might prevent his kingdom from being destroyed.

Ultimately, however, the promised military aid from the West came too little, too late. There was only a half-hearted attempt in 1444, with the pope rallying some twenty-five thousand troops to march on the Ottomans in the Balkans in what was known as the

Crusade of Varna.

But unlike the crusaders of old, who pushed the opponents of Eastern Christendom back from Constantinople's gates and descended upon the Holy Land itself, this contingent of would-be crusaders was not enough to stop the Ottoman juggernaut and was soundly defeated.

The light of the Byzantine Empire was finally snuffed out by the surging Ottoman Empire in 1453. Under Ottoman occupation, the succeeding bishops of the Eastern Orthodox Church thoroughly renounced the Council of Florence and for all that it stood. The Turkish authorities saw the division of Western and Eastern Christendom as advantageous, but there was also simmering resentment over the terms of the council, as was so vociferously expressed by Mark of Ephesus. So, despite all efforts to the contrary, the Great Schism would remain intact.

PART TWO: Reform and Resistance (1100–1800 CE)

Chapter 5: Medieval Christianity (1100–1380 CE)

The medieval period is sometimes known as the Dark Ages. This name is supposed to signify a perceived loss of some of the knowledge that had been gained during the high-water mark of antiquity. But to say that the medieval age was all dark and dreary without any hope of enlightenment would be misleading. If anything else, the Christians of the medieval period still had their faith, and for them, their faith meant everything. And their faith was not something in the abstract but a very tangible aspect of their lives.

This was demonstrated on November 27th, 1095, when Pope Urban II stood before the masses and declared that Christians needed to "take up the cross" to defend Christian interests in the East. Among the reasons given for this call to arms was to aid the Byzantine Empire, which was being hammered by Islamic forces, and to protect Christian pilgrims who had recently suffered harassment at the holy sites.

But in the minds of many medieval Christians, there was a much larger goal in mind, one that would correct what they perceived as a major wrong: the wresting of the Holy Land from the Muslim forces. Jerusalem had fallen to Islamic forces in the 7th century. At the tail end of the 11th century, Christians were rallying to take it back. Many who heard Urban II speak came to one conclusion: God wills it!

The zealous crowds chanted this phrase over and over, and this way of thinking would lead European Christians from far and wide to converge in the Middle East to take back what they believed to be theirs. Although later historians would try to cast the crusaders as nothing more than colonizers, there was more to it than that. The religiously minded people felt they were fighting for God. And a call to defend the faith could rouse folks from all walks of life to come running to join the cause.

This was perhaps best demonstrated in the so-called "People's Crusade," which was led by a lay minister and mystic called Peter the Hermit. Although the People's Crusade was not considered an official crusade as much as a mad mob of zealots, this massive wave of Christians actually reached the Levant before the First Crusade (the one that had been officially sanctioned by the pope). And the peasants of the People's Crusade met absolutely disastrous results!

This unorganized mob (and that's really what the people amounted to) was not at all trained in warfare. Nevertheless, they traipsed across Europe, causing havoc wherever they went until they somehow found themselves in Constantinople. The Greek emperor quickly washed his hands of the motley crew and allowed them to exit out his back door to the Bosporus. They made their way through Anatolia until they were utterly annihilated by the Turks who intercepted them.

Again, this was not a professional army. Just imagine a bunch of villagers armed with pitchforks, sticks, and shovels, and you get the idea. As the Turks faced this bizarre group, with scimitars cleaving through wooden staffs, they must have thought the world had gone mad. "Who were these people? And why were they here?" were likely some of the questions that came to mind.

As hard as it is for us to fathom today, these zealous medieval Christians were there because of their strong and uncompromising faith in God. It is a faith we might find utterly alien and irrational today, but this kind of unrelenting faith was very present in the Middle Ages.

At any rate, after Peter the Hermit's mob was decimated, the first official contingent of crusaders—official as in armed knights and soldiers led by kings, princes, and barons—made their way to Constantinople. Arriving at Constantinople's gates in 1097, this group was seen by the Byzantine emperor as a *real* army, so he did what he could to actively coordinate with and accommodate them.

A joint group of crusaders and Byzantines recovered the recently lost Byzantine city of Nicaea. While retaking this ancient Christian city, where the Nicene Creed was agreed upon all those years ago, the Byzantines effectively aided the crusaders, using their navy to blockade the nearby Lake Ascania so that the occupiers would be hemmed in without any hope of further aid.

The crusaders and Byzantines then hammered the Muslims from all sides until their opponents admitted defeat. Byzantine flags were soon unfurled at Nicaea once again, and the Byzantine emperor had the Latin crusaders to thank for the recovery of his lost city. At this point, the relations between the crusaders and the Byzantines were quite good, perhaps even at their highest mark, as the Byzantines were thankful for the support. They helped to lead the crusaders to their next target—Antioch.

The city of Antioch, located in the far northwestern corner of what is termed the Levant, is another ancient focal point of Christianity. Apostle Paul often used Antioch as his home base when carrying out missions farther afield in Greece and Asia Minor. In October 1097, the crusaders began their siege of Antioch. This would prove to be a long and protracted affair, with the crusaders having to hunker down for the winter. They could not take the city until the following year, in the summer of 1098.

With the conquest of Antioch, the crusaders began a pattern of refusing to honor previous pledges to return lost lands to the Byzantine Empire. Antioch had belonged to the Byzantines prior to it being taken from them by the Turks. Yet the crusaders decided to keep Antioch for themselves, beginning what would be a trend, as they would forge their own "Crusader Kingdom" in the Middle East. Antioch would form part of the larger Principality of Antioch.

The Christians marched from Antioch and reached their ultimate goal of Jerusalem in 1099. Upon their arrival, the crusaders initially could do very little, thanks to the city's immense walls. The local governor was no doubt hoping he could wait out the Christian invaders and hold on long enough for reinforcements to arrive. However, the resources within were finite and running low.

Likely due to the dwindling supplies, the governor decided to boot out all of the Christians from the city. Although the governor could be commended for not slaughtering the Christians outright, it is likely that he realized that dumping a large population of civilians on the crusaders would serve as a great distraction and further deplete the resources of his antagonists.

After all, the Christian crusaders had a duty to protect Christian civilians. But within this group of hangers-on, the crusaders found a real diamond in the rough. Among this rabble was a man known as Blessed Gerard. He was a caretaker of a local hospital and claimed to have inside knowledge as to how the crusaders could overcome the mighty walls of Jerusalem.

Gerard pointed out the most vulnerable parts of the walls and then proceeded to direct the crusaders on how best to break through them. This led to a siege tower being constructed. It was placed at one of the gates, and the crusaders were able to pour over the walls. A bloody battle ensued, with crusaders and Muslims fighting for every inch of the city. Ultimately, the crusaders prevailed, and Jerusalem—or what was left of it—was theirs to claim.

In the end, the bloodshed that occurred to obtain this prize was shocking, even to medieval sensibilities. Nevertheless, it was the foundation of what would become the Crusader States.

Now that the crusaders controlled the Holy Land, they had to figure out what to do with it. The first pressing problem was the fact that the cities and other outposts they controlled were severely understaffed. The population of Jerusalem, for example, saw a majority of its previous residents be either exalted or slaughtered. The city was a small fraction of what it had once been. There was such a shortage of personnel that many portions of the city walls went unguarded. And the situation outside of the city walls was even worse.

Christians who wished to travel to other holy sites quickly found out they were taking their lives into their own hands by doing so. The ever-present danger of being waylaid by bandits and other aggressors led to the establishment of permanent military orders to safeguard the civilian population.

The most famous of these orders would be the Knights Templar and the Knights Hospitaller. Initially tasked with safeguarding pilgrims, the various monastic orders of knights essentially became the "special forces" of the medieval period. These brave knights would give their lives for a cause that they (rightly or wrongly) believed to be bigger than their own life.

The Crusader States reached their high point in the 12th century. However, Jerusalem was lost in 1187, when the mighty Islamic commander Saladin managed to seize the capital of the Crusader States. From this point forward, the Crusader States went into decline.

The crusaders attempted to rally during the Third Crusade, which was launched in 1189. This effort was largely led by a king from England known as Richard the Lionheart. Richard would make remarkable progress and restore lost ground, but he would fall short of reclaiming Jerusalem.

The crusaders' fortunes would then go on to ebb and flow until 1291. That year, the last crusader toehold in the Holy Land—Acre—was overrun. And yes, a group of Templars, Hospitallers, and their auxiliaries defended this final outpost to the bloody, bitter end.

But on May 18th, 1291, Acre was flooded by its enemies. The city's defenders were eventually corned in the Templar House, where they positioned themselves for their final stand. Among them was a large segment of the civilian population. Many others had fled the city before it was too late, but there were still plenty of civilians who remained. They sought the safety of the Templars, Hospitallers, and other knights, all of whom swore to protect them.

The sultan grew weary of the standoff and offered to allow the civilians safe passage as long as they laid down their arms. The knights knew the battle had been lost and decided this would at least allow them to fulfill their pledge to protect the innocent. But accounts say that as soon as their antagonists entered the compound, they began to mercilessly harass the women and children.

Furious and disgusted, the knights picked their swords back up and drove their enemies from their midst, leading to a renewed standoff. This final standoff only ended when the sultan's engineers attempted to blow holes in the walls of the Templar House to gain access. The explosives were too powerful and severely damaged the foundation.

It has been said that immediately after the walls were breached and the enemy forces came pouring in, the whole structure collapsed, killing all inside. In one fell swoop, the crusaders, those under their charge, and a large portion of their opponents were all killed. It was an entirely dramatic way for the Crusades to end.

But as important as the Crusades were to medieval Christianity, they were not the only story of this age. The Western Schism, which took place in 1378, was also of great importance. This schism is not to be confused with the Great Schism of 1054, which separated the Eastern Church from the Western Church. On the contrary, the Western Schism was only within the Catholic Church. A series of popes claimed to be the sovereign of the Roman Catholic Church.

The roots of this rupture stemmed back to 1309 when Pope Clement V decided to move his papal court from Rome to the French city of Avignon because of political instability in the region at the time. However, it would set a precedent, and over the next several decades, a succession of popes would set up shop in Avignon instead of the "Eternal City."

In 1378, Pope Gregory XI decided to establish himself in Rome, just like the popes of old. This fact was resented by the clergy that had grown powerful in Avignon, and bitter backbiting between French and Roman cliques began to unfold. This set the stage for much controversy, especially when Pope Gregory XI abruptly perished that year. Gregory's immediate successor, Pope Urban VI, hailed from the Italian city of Naples.

The French clergy grew increasingly resentful and decided not to recognize the results of the papal election that brought Pope Urban VI to power. They convened in Avignon, where they held an election of their own and brought Pope Clement VII to power. He would preside over the court of Avignon, France. Of course, the Roman Catholic Church could not have two popes, so this presented an obvious dilemma for the church.

Incredibly enough, this situation persisted for about forty years, with one pope being elected in Avignon and another in Rome. Both would claim legitimacy and have their own set of cardinals in their own papal courts. And both sides would seek recognition from the various heads of state around Europe. An attempt was made to address this tumultuous situation in 1409 with the Council of Pisa.

This council determined that the only way to get things back to normal would be to cast off both current claimants and declare the popes in both Avignon and Rome as illegitimate. Then they could start anew. And that is precisely what they did. The church declared that the two popes were fake while nominating a third. However, doing such a thing was easier said than done since the popes in Avignon and Rome refused to step down.

In reality, all the Council of Pisa seemed to accomplish was additional confusion, as three popes now vied for power. The popes that were not recognized by the other factions involved would be labeled as "anti-popes," and the chaos and confusion would continue for some time.

The situation was not cleared up until 1414 when the Council of Constance was held. The pope who had been appointed at the Council of Pisa—Alexander V—had abruptly perished and was replaced by Pope John XXIII. By the time the Council of Constance was held in 1414, Pope John XXIII had fallen out of favor. He was under great pressure and distress and actually tried to escape from his handlers in 1415. However, he was ultimately rounded up, arrested, and officially removed from office. One anti-pope down; two more to go.

The next pope to be taken out was Gregory XII of Rome. The Roman pontiff saw the writing on the wall and decided it was in his best interest to step down. He issued his official resignation later that year. Benedict XIII, the pope in Avignon, tried to stick it out but was forcibly removed in July of 1417, although he continued his papacy in the Kingdom of Aragon (the only place that recognized him). Once all of the "popes" had been subdued, a new official election was held. Martin V was hailed as the one and only pope of the Roman Catholic Church.

After all of this drama came to a close, it seems the Catholic Church learned many things as it pertained to papal elections. It no doubt learned that the more one questions the results, the more trouble it creates in the long run. At any rate, throughout the subsequent centuries, most papal successions were smooth affairs. Even if there were problems, they were nowhere near the controversy that the Western Schism and its anti-popes had brought about.

Interestingly enough, the Council of Constance, which was instrumental in bringing this madness to an end, also sowed the seeds of future tumult for the Catholic Church and Christianity. During this ecumenical council, the excommunication of a great spiritual thinker by the name of Jan Hus took place.

Hus had views that did not correspond with the official doctrine of the Catholic Church. Unlike today, where folks are usually free to "agree to disagree," in the medieval period, if you lived under the dominion of the Catholic Church, any deviation from the faith could not only brand you a heretic but also lead to your death. Hus was executed for what were deemed to be contrary beliefs in regard to the sale of indulgences (the practice of donating money to the church so that certain perceived moral failings or shortcomings could be "indulged").

As we will see in the next chapter, this same criticism would form a cornerstone of Martin Luther's rebellion against the Catholic Church. Along with criticizing indulgences, Hus also took issue with many other practices of the clergy and insisted that the average Christian should have a more direct relationship with God without the need for intermediaries. Hus paid the ultimate price for his divergence of thought and was burned at the stake.

But Hus's followers, the so-called "Hussites," attempted to carry on his teachings. This would lead to the Hussite Wars, in which the Catholic Church attempted to forcibly squash the movement. More importantly, however, Jan Hus and his followers would set an example and forge a template for what would eventually become a full-fledged reformation of the Christian Church.

Chapter 6: The Protestant Reformation

As it pertains to the Protestant Reformation, the most immediate event that probably comes to mind is the action of Martin Luther nailing his *Ninety-five Theses* to the door of a church in Wittenberg. For many, this one incident seems to crystalize the call to arms to break away from the Catholic Church. But in reality, Martin Luther could hardly have foreseen how profound the fallout from his religious questioning would be.

Because yes, at the end of the day, that was all that Martin Luther was trying to do: he was simply nailing questions, arguments, and suggestions to the door of the cathedral, if that event even happened, as there is no firm evidence to suggest that it did). But regardless, the imagery has stuck, and it makes for some fun comparisons to the modern day, as Luther was like a blogger posting his thoughts for others to see. And the actions of influencers can have larger consequences than they think. When Luther he posted his *Ninety-five Theses* to the door of the cathedral, he was not trying to break away from the Catholic Church; he was simply trying to reform it.

The *Ninety-five Theses* he nailed on the door were ninety-five arguments he wished to raise with the Catholic Church, which he believed was in need of some serious reform. At the top of Martin Luther's list was the notion that the church needed to end the sale of indulgences. Indulgences were a Catholic practice for centuries.

Sinners were promised that their sins would be somehow nullified or "indulged" if they donated money to the church.

Catholics believed that the pope had the power to lessen one's time in purgatory. If one were to simply donate money to the church, the pope could indulge them or their loved ones and lessen the time that they might spend in the limbo realm of purgatory. Whether or not one believed in Catholic doctrine, the practice had become troublesome enough for many. While some of the money went to supporting charities and hospitals, most of the money went to decorating churches that were already lavish enough or into the pockets of church officials.

As mentioned in the previous chapter, the sale of indulgences had already been questioned by Jan Hus and his Hussites. Luther certainly was not the first to openly wonder whether or not this practice was being done appropriately.

There is, of course, nothing wrong with churches raising money. It makes sense that churches would accept donations since it helps keep them running and allows them to support charities. Churches of all denominations today still raise money on a regular basis. They take money from church members through the collection plate. Mega-churches might even host telethons on TV to accept funds from anyone willing to support their ministry.

The sale of indulgences was frequently used to build and maintain churches. It was not really the fact that churches accepted donations that angered Luther; it was more the way in which they solicited those donations. The priests were so systematic about it and flaunted the notion that people could practically buy their way out of purgatory, which thoroughly bothered the German monk Martin Luther.

And so, this ambitious and thoughtful theologian wanted to do something about it. Luther simply wanted to spark a discussion about current church practices and what could be done to change them. And he certainly sparked a debate. The very next day, Luther was asked to rescind the majority of his arguments.

Interestingly enough, Luther had supposedly nailed his arguments to the church door on October 31st, 1517. The following day, November 1st, was (and still is) a Catholic holiday known as All Saints' Day. October 31st was known as All Saints' Eve and, in some quarters, All Hallows' Eve. Today, of course, we know October 31st by another name: Halloween.

Martin Luther chose October 31ˢᵗ because it was the day before All Saints' Day. He knew that plenty of people would be passing through the doors of the church on that day and be able to read the notes he posted on the door. Luther was simply a savvy marketer, posting his ideas on what was akin to a bulletin board when he knew a bunch of people would be passing by.

Along with railing against indulgences, Luther's key points were about the nature of papal authority. He also argued that one was saved by faith alone with no need whatsoever for good works. Luther argued that indulgences were wrong since all one has to do to be saved was believe in Jesus Christ; a peasant did not have to pay a priest money just to have an easier afterlife. Most Christians today would probably agree with this watered-down version of Luther's thoughts.

But he was also speaking in many generalities as it pertained to the Catholic Church. Catholics did not believe that faith was insufficient; they just believed it was a continuing process. It was believed that some may not have gotten completely right with God in this life, and God was gracious enough to give them an opportunity in the afterlife by purging the process of purgatory. Just as in the Book of Maccabees, which Catholics often quoted and has the living righteous praying for the backslidden dead, Catholic belief hinged on both faith and penance in this life, as well as potential penance in the next.

Martin Luther would end up going to the other extreme, as he wished to excise the whole notion that one should do any works at all. In his later arguments, he even went as far as to suggest that the New Testament Book of James should be removed from the Bible because he took umbrage with the fact that James proclaimed, "Faith without works is dead." Martin Luther later snubbed James by calling it nothing more than an "epistle of straw."

Considering the Catholic point of view in all of this, it is pretty understandable why they looked at Luther with such contempt. The Catholics must have been thinking, "Who was this guy who thought he knew better than everyone else? Even better than Apostle James?"

In Luther's initial arguments, he refrained from criticizing the pope outright. He leveled his primary blame on his subordinates. Luther even stated that he was certain that the pontiff would fix the issues he brought up if he knew about them. The pope would soon learn all about Martin Luther, and there would be consequences for Luther's actions.

Regardless of whether you agree with his theological criticisms or not, one must hand it to Luther for his boldness. In Martin Luther's day, it was not common to openly criticize the church in this manner. Others had lost their lives for less stinging criticism. However, Luther had an ace up his sleeve. He was in good with the local German ruler, the Elector of Saxony, Frederick the Wise.

A little bit of background is required to understand this figure. As mentioned previously in this book, for several centuries, a conglomeration of central and western European states known as the Holy Roman Empire existed. Although Martin Luther was German, spoke German, and wrote German, the nation-state of Germany did not yet exist. It would not exist until 1871.

Back during the Reformation, Germany was a large chunk of the Holy Roman Empire. The interesting thing about the Holy Roman Empire is that it had developed a system of electing its emperors. Scattered throughout the Holy Roman Empire were electors who made up a college, which had the final say in who would become the Holy Roman emperor.

If you are from the United States, the notion of electors serving an integral part of an election likely sounds familiar to you. This is no coincidence. The Founding Fathers of the United States scoured the globe for inspiration when they crafted the framework of how the US should function.

At any rate, in the Holy Roman Empire, these electors wielded formidable power, and no one wanted to get on their bad side. Fortunately for Martin Luther, he was on the good side of the elector of Saxony. So, as much as the pope might have wanted to burn Luther as a heretic, he dared not do so lest he anger this crucial component of the Holy Roman Empire. And Frederick's importance only grew when the sitting head of the Holy Roman Empire, Maximilian I, passed away in January 1519.

Maximilian's grandson was the leading claimant to be the next Holy Roman emperor. But again, even though he was favored, the position was not a straightforward hereditary role. Charles V still had to make sure he received enough backing from all of the electors to ensure his seat on the throne. For this reason, both Charles V and the pope were unwilling to risk alienating Luther's benefactor, the elector of Saxony.

And this was the real reason behind Luther's success. He had a powerful political backer that ensured he would be able to continue to speak his mind. And when Luther was assailed by a prominent Catholic theologian by the name of John Eck, he decided to strike back. He entered into an angry literary exchange with Eck, in which both trounced each other and each other's views.

At one point, Luther even referred to Eck as being nothing more than "an irritated prostitute." All of these angry words culminated in a face-to-face debate in Leipzig in June 1519. During this debate, Luther argued against the infallibility of the pope or any human being and instead urged Christians to depend upon the infallible word of God.

Luther's argument sounds great on the surface. He was basically saying not to worry about the pope's interpretation of things but to open up a Bible and draw your own conclusions (at least, that is, those who were able to read). It was this line of thinking that would create an explosion of countless Protestant denominations, as just about everyone had their own interpretation of just about everything, from how to perform a baptism and Communion to what it actually meant to be saved.

These differences in opinion would ultimately spark bloody persecution and all-out wars, not just between Catholics and Protestants but also between various Protestant denominations that would battle it out to see whose interpretation was "best." This religious persecution led the Pilgrims to pile into the *Mayflower* and head to North America. They were not persecuted by Catholics but by other Protestants.

So, as noble as Luther's efforts might have been, he was truly opening Pandora's box by inviting people other than the pope and trained clergy to interpret the scripture. The Council of Nicaea had been held centuries before to create a universal interpretation of the scripture and a universal creed, yet Martin blew all of that to bits when he gave freedom to himself and his fellow Protestants to interpret the scripture in any way they saw fit.

As had been the case in the 1st and 2nd centuries, matters that had been deemed long settled by the church were now suddenly open for debate. Even Martin Luther, in his later years, would get into heated arguments with other Protestants over just what the scriptures meant. So, playing devil's advocate for the Catholic Church, one can certainly understand why the Catholics might blame Martin Luther for being the source of all of this chaos and confusion.

At any rate, Eck predictably insisted that the pope, as the head of the church, be trusted as the supreme director of the faith. Luther dissented, bringing up the Great Schism of 1054. He pointed out that the Greeks of the Orthodox East had been happy for centuries, and they did not listen to the pope. Luther was still being subtle in his dissent at this point, but in his private writings, he was already referring to the pope as the greatest enemy of Christianity.

After the debate ended, the backlash against Luther was palpable. Many universities began to burn his works and castigated the bold monk for his statements. The ax finally fell in 1520 when the pope sent a papal bull that found forty errors in Luther's beliefs. He gave Luther sixty days to personally appear in Rome to answer for them. If Luther refused to do so, he would be promptly excommunicated.

Despite all of his previous hubris, this was a grim and desperate moment for Martin Luther. He really only had three choices, and all of them would have dramatic consequences. He could choose to go to Rome and throw himself at the pope's feet while begging for forgiveness and promising to correct the "error" of his ways. Even if he decided to do such a thing, there was no guarantee that his image would be fully rehabilitated. If Luther were anything less than penitent and submissive, the outcome likely would not have been good.

Needless to say, if he showed up in Rome and shook his finger in the pope's face and declared the pope to be the anti-Christ, he likely would not have fared too well either. Ultimately, Luther took the third option: he did not go to Rome at all.

This option, of course, meant that after the sixty days were up, he would be officially excommunicated from the church. By deciding to ignore the summons, Luther knew there would be no turning back. He was deemed an enemy of the Catholic Church. Luther was not one to do anything halfway. He decided that if he was the pope's opponent that he would make sure he was the best opponent the pontiff ever had.

As soon as the sixty days had passed, rather than grieve, Luther celebrated. He and his supporters even started a bonfire, tossing the papal bull and other Catholic books into the flames. The pope pushed back more vigorously on January 3rd, 1521, by officially declaring the excommunication of Luther and all who followed him.

In the meantime, the Holy Roman Empire had successfully elected Charles V, who was a staunch Catholic. Charles V convened the famous Diet of Worms and ordered the renegade monk, Martin Luther, to attend. Luther was still being guaranteed protection by the elector of Saxony, so other than another round of condemnations by Catholic theologians, there was really nothing more that anyone could do to him. The Diet of Worms was held on April 17th, 1521.

The meeting was held with great fanfare, and people gathered from miles around. Initially, Luther was shaken up a bit by the high-profile members of the diet. He ended up asking for more time to consider how to answer questions presented to him. Luther was given another day to think everything over, and he returned on the 18th, visibly more relaxed and ready to play ball.

Although Luther admitted that he had perhaps gone a bit too far with some of his rhetoric, especially as it pertained to personally attacking other religious leaders, he stood by the key tenants of his beliefs. Luther managed to get on the bad side of Holy Roman Emperor Charles V. But Charles was cautious enough not to upset the elector of Saxony, so he held his punches.

Charles V did not go as far as to order any harm done to Martin Luther, but he did officially declare his own personal belief that Martin Luther was a heretic. Although no official call was made to seize Luther, the fact that he had been disparaged by such important figures put his personal safety into question, as any would-be Catholic vigilante might decide to take him out.

As such, Luther knew that he had to tread very carefully. He decided to hide in the friendly confines of Wartburg Castle and even temporarily changed his identity to Junker Jörg or, as it would be rendered in English, Knight George.

In the meantime, Luther's supporters at Wittenberg continued the reform that Martin Luther had begun. Other leaders of the Reformation would emerge elsewhere, such as in Switzerland with the rise of Ulrich Zwingli in 1522. Zwingli's initial form of protest might seem almost comical, but it drove home a point. He simply told his followers to eat some "sausage." The Catholic Church had a tradition of not eating meat just before the advent of Easter (this period is also known as Lent). Zwingli wanted to poke holes in all manner of Catholic traditions, so he began with this one. One can almost imagine him shouting aloud, "The pope does not want us to eat meat before Easter, so let's have some sausages!"

It sounds patently absurd, but this is essentially how Zwingli's major movement toward reform first gained steam. And Zwingli was deadly serious about his beliefs. He was serious enough to fight for them. This Protestant reformer ended up perishing at the head of a literal army in 1531. If Catholics feared that all hell would break loose if folks just haphazardly interpreted the scripture any way they chose, this would have been a perfect moment for them to have pointed the finger and declared, "I told you so!"

The Anabaptists of Switzerland also squabbled and came to blows over the proper means of baptism. They argued against the Catholic practice of baptizing babies and were willing to die for this belief. Many of them did. The city of Zurich began cracking down on the Anabaptists, and in their persecution, many were rounded up and forcibly drowned out of anger over the practice of baptism.

Many Anabaptists would flee to the United States, where they founded communities. Their descendants still carry out their traditions in Mennonite and Amish communities.

These were some of the initial main reformers of the Protestant Reformation, but more reforms would soon follow, especially in France and England.

Chapter 7: Religious Reform in France and England

France's reformation may have come a little later than that of Germany, Switzerland, and other regions, but it was just as powerful. The French Reformation was led by a firebrand French preacher by the name of John Calvin. Calvin was a little younger than Luther at the time of his rise to prominence, and it is perhaps his youthful exuberance that explains his willingness to push things much further than Martin Luther ever dared to do.

Martin Luther had carefully pried open the door for change, and radicals like Calvin were the ones who charged right through the open doorway. John Calvin began his life in the French town of Picardy, just north of Paris. His family was a prominent one, so they were sure to give their son a good education. They sent him off to the University of Paris, where he initially set out to study law. Calvin switched gears after his dad passed away, deciding to study Hebrew and Greek instead.

He developed his skills in the two main languages of the Bible, which would allow him to better understand the intricate interpretations of the scripture. After the Reformation erupted, Calvin began to apply this knowledge to his own interpretations of religion. By the 1530s, Calvin had become fully devoted to the cause of religious reform. However, as a leader of religious dissent, things became a bit too difficult for him in Paris, with the king of France deciding to push back against religious reform. This prompted Calvin to run off to Basel, Switzerland.

Switzerland, which had been the launching pad for Zwingli, was already a powerful bastion for reformers. Calvin sought refuge here, heading to the Protestant town of Strasbourg before setting up shop in Geneva. In Geneva, in 1536, Calvin published his famous work, *Institutes of the Christian Religion.*

Here, Calvin set forth his beliefs. Chief among them was the idea that the true knowledge of God could only be gained from one's own interpretation of the Bible. According to Calvin, one could not find God through reason and logic but instead needed a personal connection to the word of God. Furthermore, unlike Martin Luther, who at times wished to excise various books of the Bible that did not line up with his own viewpoints, Calvin insisted that all of the scripture was sacred and that none of it should be omitted.

He also put a much heavier emphasis on the Old Testament than other reformers. But the most famous belief Calvin developed was his notion that everything was preordained. He believed that God, being omniscient, must know in advance who would gain salvation and who would turn their back on their creator. This theory of everyone being predestined for either salvation or damnation would become known as "predestination," and it became a key Calvinist belief.

In many ways, Calvin's idea of predestination makes sense. If God is an omniscient, all-powerful being outside of space and time, it makes sense that he would know how everything would play out. It would be like one of us sitting in front of a cartoon strip and being able to clearly see the beginning and the end of it.

For some, this creates a problem because they feel it negates free will. But really, it just depends on your interpretation. A Calvinist does not believe that we are all pre-programmed robots that God set in motion. We still have free will, and it is still us making choices. But God is literally outside of space, time, and all human experience, so Calvinists believe he already knows what we are all going to do.

If one were to dig even deeper, one could find scripture to bolster this argument. The New Testament champions the idea that God knew that Adam and Eve would choose to rebel against him ahead of time, stating that Christ was the "Lamb slain from the foundation of the world" (Revelation 13:8).

At any rate, when this notion that God knew from the very beginning who would do what was presented to the masses, this teaching caused quite a bit of consternation and chaos. And it wasn't just people outside of the Calvinist fold. Suddenly, Calvinists became utterly consumed with trying to figure out which side of the predestination scales they might be on. They went on frantic, neurotic quests to figure out whether or not they were destined to be saved or doomed to be damned. This worry and fear caused so much consternation in the Calvinist movement that steps had to be made to encourage all Calvinist believers to stop worrying over their predestination and simply do all they could to live a good Christian life.

Yes, what should have been the goal of all Christians in the first place had to be painstakingly reintroduced to the Calvinists so they could once again sleep peacefully at night. It makes one appreciate the biblical admonition to "lean not to your own understanding" (Proverbs 3:5). It seems that every time a great thinker of the Reformation introduced a bold new understanding of scripture, the Protestant masses erupted in chaos, as they were confused or worried about how that belief impacted them.

After some of the confusion of predestination died down, Calvin was able to establish a strong church hierarchy in Geneva, complete with pastors, teachers, elders, and deacons. These were the "fourfold ministry" that Calvin believed to have been revealed by the scripture. To Calvin's credit, Geneva soon became what has been termed a model Christian commonwealth. The success of Geneva would serve as an inspiration to others, including the growing Protestant movement in England.

England was a different beast when it came to public sentiment and the attitudes of the royals. England had some upswelling of Protestantism, but by and large, the majority of the English were still Catholic. And more importantly, their king, Henry VIII, was a very staunch Catholic. In fact, King Henry had been dubbed the "Defender of the Faith" by the pope. He earned this title by publishing writing that railed against Martin Luther and condemned the Reformation.

Henry had no problem at all with Catholic belief until the pope's authority crimped his style as it pertained to his personal life. You see,

Henry desperately wanted a son, as he wanted a male heir to succeed him on the throne. His first wife, Catherine of Aragon, seemed unable to give him one. So, Henry wished for an annulment. As Catholic tradition dictated, he had to look to the pope for permission.

Granting such an annulment would have been no easy thing for the pope since Henry's wife was Holy Roman Emperor Charles V's aunt! The pope knew that if he granted the annulment, he would have to deal with Charles V's wrath. However, the pope did not wish to anger either monarch. He tried to play out the clock, not giving a direct answer either way. But as the pope dithered, it became clearer to Henry that he would not get what he wanted. So, King Henry began to turn his back on the pope.

The first real break occurred in 1534 when King Henry issued an edict known as the Act of Supremacy, which sought to negate the pope's authority. Henry declared himself the supreme head of the Church of England. In other words, Henry had officially broken away from the Catholic Church. And as Henry began to turn away from the papacy, English reformers, such as Thomas Cromwell and Thomas Cranmer, began to come to prominence as they advocated for change. However, for the most part, the Church of England was very similar to the Catholic Church.

Henry had his own problems to deal with, though. He married another woman, Anne Boleyn (the two actually married in 1533, the same year Thomas Cranmer annulled his marriage to Catherine of Aragon). His new wife proved just as unable to give him the son he so desperately craved. Infuriated, Henry put away his wife and had her beheaded on trumped-up charges of sedition. Henry then married a woman named Jane Seymour, who succeeded where others had failed, giving birth to a boy named Edward. To Henry's great grief, his beloved Jane perished shortly afterward.

Even so, the widowed Henry did not take long to remarry, wedding Anne of Cleves next. This marriage would be incredibly brief. After just a few months, Henry backed out of it, using his newfound powers over the church and state to render this latest marriage null and void.

Henry then went on to marry a lady named Catherine Howard. She would be accused of adultery and lost her head. And finally, Henry married Catherine Parr, who would stay by Henry's side until he died.

King Henry was aghast at some of the reforms taking place in his own backyard, and the old "defender of the faith" decided to take a stand against the multiple interpretations of scripture that were being made.

He issued another edict, the Act for the Advancement of True Religion. This act apparently took up the old biblical injunction to "lean to your own understanding," as it stated that there should be limits on who had access to scripture so that folks would not run around developing a multiplicity of ideas.

Just like the Catholic Church, Henry wished to make sure his subjects stuck to the same doctrine and interpretation rather than drawing their own conclusions. The fact that King Henry had broken from the pope yet still sought to take similar measures of control that the Catholic Church had sworn by for centuries led many Protestant reformers to understandably grumble that the reforms were not going far enough.

But after King Henry's passing in 1547, the reformers would have their chance to reshape religion in England. The country would ultimately become largely Protestant-leaning as a result, especially under Queen Elizabeth I.

PART THREE: Key Christian Themes

Chapter 8: Catholic Saints

The Catholic Church has long been known for its adoration of saints. It is a source of great pride for those who adhere to the Catholic faith while also often being a source of derision for those who do not. Catholics are sometimes derided by Protestants for praying to dead saints, but Catholics take pride in their belief that the venerable spirits of the saints who have left this mortal coil can still be a source of good in this world today.

The first great saint of the Catholic Church—at least of those outside of the official biblical canon—is no doubt the theological giant Saint Augustine of Hippo. Saint Augustine lived during a pivotal time, during the 5th century when the traditional Roman Empire was in decline. Rome was being threatened on all sides, and at one point, it was even sacked.

Augustine wrote his epic work *On the City of God Against the Pagans* to explain why such things might happen. At first glance at the title of his treatise, one might think that Augustine was promoting Rome as the city of God. But this was not the case. Augustine was instead urging Catholics to lift their eyes away from Rome and look toward the eternal "City of God," which had not yet been experienced by humanity.

Augustine was pivotal in fashioning much of what the Catholic Church would crystalize as its official doctrine. Interestingly enough, Augustine had something for the later Calvinists who believed in predestination and those who abhorred them because it seemed to erase the concept of free will. As it turns out, all the way back in the 5th century, Augustine wrote that "God orders all things while preserving human freedom."

Yes, Augustine believed in the omniscience of God's knowledge and the agency of human freedom to fulfill what God essentially already knows. Saint Augustine had views on original sin, grace, and the nature of evil, which would be highly influential on the Roman Catholic Church. Augustine also had some intriguing views about the nature of God and the state of time and space.

Augustine was one of the first to suggest that God was literally outside of space and time. He explained eternity to be a timeless state outside of the human timeframe as we know it. Augustine was obviously a deep thinker, and his mind frequently plumbed the depths of the greatest mysteries of existence.

But at the end of the day, Augustine knew that certain questions could not be answered, but he still could not help but wonder. He never lost his sense of wonder or his sense of humor when considering the nature of creation. On one occasion, he made what was perhaps one of the greatest wisecracks of any great Catholic theologian.

He was musing about people who might ask what God was doing before creation. Yes, what was the creator of the universe up to before the universe was created? The idea seems hopelessly unanswerable and even absurd. *What was God doing?* Can we picture the creator just kicking back, taking it easy?

Augustine had a great answer to this question. When he was asked what God was doing before creation, he suggested, "Preparing hell for those who pry too deep!" as if there was a special compartment of purgatory for folks who were too inquisitive for their own good. All joking aside, Augustine was as inquisitive as anyone, and he relished pondering mysteries on a regular basis.

Another Catholic saint who was highly influential was Thomas Aquinas. Thomas Aquinas was steeped in his Catholic faith and had been gifted with a powerful sense of logic and deductive reasoning. Aquinas was a follower of the ancient Greek philosopher Aristotle and sought to apply the wisdom of such ancient thinkers to his day and age.

His penchant for ancient philosophers occasionally got him in trouble with his religious peers, but by and large, the genius of his synthesis has come to be recognized. The interesting thing about Aquinas was that he believed many aspects of life could be figured out through reason. However, he did acknowledge that logic and reason were insufficient to realize the most profound mysteries of life, such as the nature of God and the origin of the universe.

Aquinas believed that for the most unfathomable of questions, logic fell short and that only faith and divine revelation could suffice. In pondering the greatest of mysteries, Aquinas also listed five positive statements about the nature of God. Aquinas stated that "God is simple, without composition of parts, such as body and soul, or matter and form. God is perfect, lacking nothing. God is infinite, and not limited in the ways that created beings are physically, intellectually, and emotionally limited. God is immutable, incapable of change in respect of essence and character. God is one, such that God's essence is the same as God's existence."

Aquinas also argued over what he saw as five rational proofs for the existence of God. One of his most famous was the notion that there was an "unmoved mover." "Everything that is moved is moved by a mover, therefore there is an unmoved mover from whom all motion proceeds, which is God." Aquinas saw the universe in motion and rationally deduced that something must have caused it to go into motion. In his mind, it made sense that the mover would be the still, unchangeable, unmovable God.

Another great figure of the Catholic Church was Saint Francis of Assisi. Saint Francis hailed from a wealthy family and began life as a seeker of material comfort. However, he would reach a crossroads as a young man, as he would have visions of God telling him to "rebuild the church."

Francis gave up his material wealth and began to live a life of monkish modesty. He initially took the commands he heard of rebuilding the church as literal ones. At one point, Francis was begging on the street for stones and other building materials to help repair a dilapidated local church. Francis would start his own order of monks and came to realize that he was meant to rebuild not just a building but also the entire framework of the Roman Catholic Church.

There are many interesting anecdotal tales of Francis's gentleness and kindness. He is especially known for his love for animals. Francis was said to have been able to literally commune with nature. He stood in the wilderness preaching to birds and other woodland creatures.

There is also an interesting tale about when a wolf attacked local villagers. The villagers wanted to hunt down and kill the beast, but Francis supposedly went right up to the wolf and soothed the animal with just a few words. Thereafter, the wolf was as tame as a dog and a favorite pet of the village.

Whereas theological giants like Augustine and Aquinas are known for their treatises, Aquinas is remembered and relished as a man who was a living example of what a good Christian should be. Through his own personal actions, he demonstrated the great depth of God's love.

Chapter 9: Religious Expansion and Global Outreach

The expedition that led to the European discovery of the Americas in 1492 had religion as one of its catalysts. Spain had long been waging a bloody Reconquista to reclaim territories that had previously been seized by Islamic armies. In 1492, the very last Muslim enclave of Grenada had been conquered by the Spaniards, bringing the Reconquista to a close.

The Reconquista was immediately followed by one of the darkest periods in Christian history: the Inquisition. There would be several versions of the Inquisition, with the main ones taking place in Spain, Rome, and Portugal. Spain would largely be ground zero for religious intolerance of the worst kind.

Just prior to the close of the Reconquista, Spain had been a multicultural/multireligious melting pot of Jews, Christians, and Muslims. However, once the Christian powers retook the Iberian Peninsula, they were determined to make sure that Christianity was the unquestioned religion of the land. Jews, subsequently known as "conversos," were forced to convert, as were the Muslims, who were known as "moriscos."

But ultimately, these forced conversions were not good enough for the Christian authorities, who suspected that many of these conversions were false. So, in 1492, an inquisition—or inquiry—was made into who was a Christian and who was not. In the first wave of the Spanish Inquisition, which was kickstarted in 1492, Jews and conversos were mercilessly targeted, leading to torture, death, and a massive expulsion.

Spanish monarchs Ferdinand and Isabella, who were responsible for starting the Spanish Inquisition, financed Christopher Columbus to set sail to find a westward passage to Asia (as you might already know, money and new resources were also major catalysts for discovering the Americas). However, Columbus and his crew were not looking to find the Americas; they inadvertently stumbled upon the Caribbean islands. Columbus would go to his deathbed thinking he had sailed to India, but the enormity of the discovery would soon be realized and exploited.

There were those looking for monetary gain in the New World, but there were also those who were avidly seeking converts. Missions soon popped up all over the New World, and the Catholic doctrine, as well as the languages of Spanish and Portuguese, were being vigorously taught to the inhabitants. New World settlements began in the Caribbean and then moved to Mexico, Central America, and South America.

Everywhere the Europeans went, they brought the cross, the sword, and diseases. One of the most dramatic instances of forced conversion happened during the toppling of the Aztec Empire in Mexico. The Aztecs had a religious system in place that the Spanish conquistadors viewed as appalling. And to be fair, Aztec religious practices would be appalling to modern sensibilities as well.

Unless you are a fan of human sacrifice, you likely would not have enjoyed what the Aztec priests did. The Aztecs had a long-held tradition of a priest standing on top of one of their majestic temples and ripping out the still-beating heart of a sacrificial victim. The blood of this poor victim would stream down the grand steps of the temple for all to see.

What was the reason for all of this? The Aztecs believed that if they did not engage in daily human sacrifice, the sun would cease to rise and set, and the world would come to an end. More specifically, they believed that a hungry sun god by the name of Huitzilopochtli needed fresh blood and human hearts to ensure that the sun could travel across the skies unhindered.

It is unclear how and when they convinced themselves of such a thing. We also are not sure how often these sacrifices took place.

The Aztecs were a mighty force in the region, and at the time of the Spanish conquest, they had brought just about every neighboring tribe under their dominion. It has been theorized that as the power of the Aztecs grew, the human sacrifices took on not only a religious meaning but also a political or psychological one.

At any rate, by the time the Spanish arrived on the scene, the Aztecs were apparently sacrificing folks in great vigor, although it is possible the Spanish saw one or two ceremonies and assumed that the Aztecs did it daily. When the Christians saw such a thing in practice, it was quite easy for them to peg the Aztecs as a bunch of heretics of the worst sort. So, it is really no surprise when these religious zealots from Iberia engineered the downfall of the Aztecs and instituted a colonial Catholic government in its place.

But the conquest of the conquistadors is perhaps not as dramatic as it is sometimes presented. The key to their success was toppling the leadership of those they conquered. The Aztec imperial line had been extinguished. Additionally, the Aztec leaders had been quite ruthless to the common people over which they ruled. The average citizen's life was not easy. As such, it was fairly easy for the Spanish to convince the population, especially those from rival tribes, that the abolition of this government they did not like (and did not want to be sacrificed for) was in their best interest.

If the Aztec government had been popular with the average citizen, one could imagine a prolonged guerilla war and a much greater struggle. But this was not the case. After the downfall of the Aztec government, some of the local indigenous people flocked to the Spaniards' religion, Christianity. Perhaps helping them in their decision to leave their old faith was the pure and simple fact that the world didn't end.

After the Spaniards ended the practice of human sacrifice, it became quite clear to the indigenous people that the sun continued to rise and set. It was also clear that the Aztec leaders had either lied to them or were incredibly deluded. Considering as much, it is no wonder that the new religion of Christianity might have seemed appealing to them.

But to say that all indigenous people immediately gravitated toward Christianity would be false. There were plenty of locals who resented the religion that had been foisted upon them. There were also some instances of violent rebellions against religious enforcers. The most common form of rebellion was much more subtle and involved fusing indigenous beliefs with Christianity.

This fusion of cultures was probably best demonstrated in the vision of the Virgin of Guadalupe. Around 1531, in Mexico City, the Virgin Mary was supposedly seen by some of the local populace. Rather than scoffing at such a thing, the local Catholic authorities were impressed. They believed in the absolute sincerity of those who told them of the vision, and it became an established miracle of the Catholic Church. At the forefront of much of the religious undertaking in the New World was the Jesuits. The Jesuits were founded by the visionary and mystic Saint Ignatius of Loyola and were determined to establish missions throughout the New World, which would serve as focal points of the faith. The Iberian cousins of the Spaniards, the Portuguese, also made great efforts to convert the natives.

The Portuguese not only founded Brazil in South America but also several outposts in Africa and Asia. The Portuguese famously sailed all the way to India in 1498, stating that they were in search of "spices and Christians." It might seem a rather odd statement to make, but many Europeans had heard rumors of Christian communities existing in the Far East, and these Portuguese explorers wished to find them.

And they did find a small isolated community of Christians that supposedly dated all the way back to the efforts of Apostle Thomas, who allegedly traveled to the Far East. The Portuguese went on to establish an outpost in India called Goa. This would become a trading outpost and a forward base for the spreading of Catholicism.

The Jesuits would play a major role in the outpost of Goa as well, as Jesuit mission leader Francis Xavier would arrive on the scene in the early 1500s. Francis worked with a group of locals known as the Paravas, who lived in fishing communities on the coast. This group had seen massive conversions and showed an interest early on. Xavier worked to increase their understanding of the Catholic faith, teaching them the proper use of sacraments and the Nicene Creed. Xavier's efforts were quite successful, and he carried on his work in Sri Lanka and eventually Japan.

The missionary efforts of Catholics were indeed aggressive during this period, but the Protestants would not go unchallenged. However, their approach would be markedly different. The Protestant missionary outreach often worked seemingly in reverse of the Catholic one.

While the Catholic missionaries usually had the official backing of the Vatican and their national governments, the Protestants were more likely to be fleeing from their governments. Some of the first North American colonies were founded in an attempt to set up religious societies free from the control of the English Crown. Some would even refer to these outposts as "shining cities on a hill" in reference to Christ's words in the New Testament that likened Christians to much the same thing—a light for all the world to see and pattern themselves after.

A group of religious diehards known as the Puritans, named for their notions of keeping their faith and religious practices pure and true to form, made their way to North America in large numbers in the 1630s. They sought religious freedom and came in massive numbers; some historians have dubbed it the "swarming of the Puritans."

Since they were far away from England and its control, they were able to set up their own version of society, which they called the "Holy Commonwealth." The first governor of this commonwealth—John Winthrop—was the one who made the famous notion of America being a "shining city on a hill." Winthrop would go down in history as stating, "We must consider that we shall be as a city upon a hill, the eyes of all the people are upon us."

These religious pilgrims knew that everyone was watching their little project and that it was up to them to make sure that it was successful. The Puritans lived and breathed the scripture, and they likened themselves to the "Children of Israel," a reference to the Old Testament of the Bible, with whom God had made a covenant. The Puritans felt that they had been given a special charter by the Almighty to establish themselves in a new land.

Of course, we must remember that this land was already inhabited. But unlike the brutal conquest of the conquistadors, these religious pilgrims would not initially take their lands through violence. There were certainly conflicts in this early stage of colonization, but it was not on the scale of what was being done in Mexico and Central and South America. These religious pilgrims were not hellbent on conquering people. That was not why they came to North America.

The widescale oppression of Native Americans in North America would not occur until an official government structure was established and standing armies were brought over, which would slowly push the Native Americans westward. And the next wave of religious pilgrims from England—the Quakers—were even more pacificist than the Puritans.

In the late 1600s, led by William Penn, this group of religious freedom seekers would end up founding Pennsylvania. It is well known that William Penn had excellent relations with neighboring Native American tribes. In line with Quaker beliefs, Penn believed that all human beings had a spark of God within them, something the Quakers called the "inner light of God."

In that sense, everyone was naturally united as brothers and sisters of creation. And it is no coincidence that Penn named the capital of what would become Pennsylvania "Philadelphia." This was a reference to the older Greek city of the same name, but the meaning of the name also reflects Penn's values. The Greek translation of "Philadelphia" is "city of brotherly love."

After Penn passed away in 1718, relations began to break down, and a long, sad history of bloodshed and oppression would erupt. The interesting thing about William Penn and the Quakers is that they displayed a surprising degree of religious tolerance. Although they were quite serious about their own personal beliefs, they did not believe in forcing them on others. The Quakers felt that if one were to accept religious truths, one had to accept them of their own accord; they could not be forced down people's throats.

So, unlike the Puritans, who were hellbent on "purifying" the religious beliefs of others, the Quakers invited all manner of religious denominations to live in their communities. The Quaker faithful had been persecuted back in England (and they were persecuted to an extent in the New World), so they knew how important religious tolerance was.

One of the persecuted denominations of Europe who found refuge in Pennsylvania was the German-speaking Anabaptists. These people would later become known as the Pennsylvania Dutch.

France, in the meantime, would remain staunchly Catholic, although, by the 1700s, there was an increasingly popular movement known as Deism. The Deists believed that there must be some sort of higher power, but they believed that the evidence for this supreme being was available to all simply by looking at nature itself. Even before any knowledge of the "big bang theory," Deists were convinced that the universe could not have just popped into existence from nothing and that there must be a creating agent behind it. It is simple but profound logic. We exist; therefore, there must have been something that made us exist.

However, the Deists did not believe in what they termed "manmade religion." The Deists sought to tear down what they viewed as artificial, manmade constructs when considering this omniscient deity. The Deists sought to broaden the horizons of conventional faith. It has often been said that the movement toward Deism could have been a direct consequence of previous missionary outreaches to far-flung parts of the globe.

As Christian missionaries sought to "enlighten" various peoples of other religions, some of these missionaries came away from the exchange as the ones receiving enlightenment. In other words, the religious and mystical ideas of other religions began to convince some Christians that there were real kernels of wisdom available in other faiths. And if other faiths could be so wise, was that not proof that the creator had shown himself in countless ways to countless people all over the world? Those were the sort of questions that a Deist would ask.

Rather than believing in the New Testament scripture that states the path to heaven (enlightenment) is a narrow one, the Deists began to believe that enlightenment was essentially on top of a mountain. And there were several winding roads that might lead one to the top. French writer Voltaire was a famous proponent of Deism, and after the French Revolution, many French intellectuals became Deists. The notorious general-turned-dictator Napoleon Bonaparte was known for his Deist beliefs.

Back in North America in the 18th century, a religious revival was occurring under John Wesley and his Methodists. The Methodists, just like the Puritans and the Quakers, did not name their own movement. Just like their predecessors, their names began as derisive epithets that were given to them by their opponents. Those who did not appreciate the efforts of Wesley and his followers sarcastically called them "Methodists" because Wesley had prescribed methods for prayer, fasting, praise, and everything in between.

And just like many other derided faiths, the Methodists took what was meant as an insult and wore it as a badge of honor. Yes, they would come to be proud of their peculiar methodology and sought to spread their Methodist notions far and wide. Major progress was made in 1784 when Wesley appointed a man by the name of Thomas Coke as bishop.

Around the same time, the passionate evangelism of Henry Alline was gaining notice in the northern reaches of Canada. Alline spoke from the heart, and his evangelical fervor would become known as evangelicalism.

Evangelicalism was opposed to what was viewed as the cold logic and reasoning of previous movements, such as the Calvinists and Puritans. This movement was more about personal experiences and one's connection to God rather than methodical reasoning. Alline's evangelicals would soon spread farther south, and the so-called "evangelical movement" would become one of the main threads in the tapestry of American Christianity. It has been argued that the American Revolution kicked off just as the evangelical movement first gained steam. It has been suggested that evangelical calls for freedom of expression were another factor in stimulating the cause for making a final break with England.

All of these religious movements in North America began with religious freedom in mind, and they would be in prime position after the American Revolution came to an official close in 1783. All would be prepped and primed for further religious growth as the new century of the 1800s dawned.

PART FOUR: Modern Christianity (1800–Present Day)

Chapter 10: The Many Faces of Christianity and the Separation of Church and State

Although at various times, Christian authority figures have attempted to suppress new strands of interpretation, there has always been a multiplicity of faces of the Christian faith. This potential for multiple interpretations has always been a source of strength and a source of conflict in the Christian Church.

During the 1st and 2nd centuries, religious views were extremely diverse. This diversity often led to confusion. If just about every sect had a different view of the divinity of Christ, what was one to believe? The desire for the uniformity of the faith and a so-called "universal" or "Catholic" church led Emperor Constantine to call for the Council of Nicaea, in which a standard and uniform doctrine was encapsulated within the Nicene Creed.

The creed was the glue that held Christian beliefs together for centuries, with only one great crack occurring in 1054 when the Eastern Church and Western Church split. The Western Church would hold the faith together quite well until a German monk by the name of Martin Luther called for reform. His teachings on reform and, most importantly, justification by faith alone sent shockwaves through the Catholic Church.

The Reformation led to new splinter groups of Christian belief. Initially, the Protestants predominantly hailed from the far northern reaches of Europe. It is interesting to note that the oldest bastions of Catholicism in southern Europe, such as Spain, Portugal, France, and Italy, would remain Catholic while those countries that had more recently converted to Christianity in the far north (just think of the Norse Vikings of Scandinavia) were the quickest to switch from Catholicism to Protestantism.

Many faces of Christianity developed, and these faces would soon find themselves taking up shop in the New World and farther afield, with Christian expansion reaching a global level. Although Mexico, Central America, and South America would be the "beneficiaries" of a massive conversion program to Catholicism, North America remained an interesting experiment in the diversity of religion. North America would not have one predominant Christian religion; rather, it would be home to a multitude of Christian faiths.

The sheer diversity of religious beliefs in North America led the Founding Fathers of what would become the United States to make freedom of religion an important tenant of the Constitution. The idea that the government should not infringe upon one's own personal beliefs would lead the United States down the road of what would become known as the separation of church and state.

Thomas Jefferson, a Founding Father who wrote the Declaration of Independence, viewed the long history of conflicts over rather trivial religious differences. He famously stated that the religious beliefs of the individual "neither picks my pocket nor breaks my leg." In other words, as long as religion stayed in the private sector and state law stayed out of religion, then the government could just focus on being an able and just administrator. And as long as no one infringed on the rights of someone else and followed the laws of the nation, one should be allowed to have their own personal beliefs.

This strain of thought emerged in the US Constitution's First Amendment, which, along with ensuring free speech and several other freedoms, also insisted on the freedom of religion. Unlike many of America's European predecessors, there would be no established national religion in the United States. Still, for a country steeped in Christianity, it was not always easy to find that sweet spot of neutrality.

In an effort to find more neutral footing, many of the Founding Fathers looked toward ancient Greece and Rome for inspiration. It is for this reason that so many aspects of the US capital reflect the civic symbols of antiquity, as they were largely a means of moving away from the polarizing aspects of religion. These symbols, of course, predate Christianity and can be viewed as being neutral or even ambiguous.

Just think of the back of a US dollar bill. There are no crosses or other religious symbols but vague symbolism, such as pyramids, obelisks, and eagles. And contrary to popular belief, the phrase "In God We Trust" was added to US currency recently. The phrase was approved under the Eisenhower administration and did not appear on paper money until 1957.

Much of the inspiration for putting this phrase on money back then was said to have been out of a surge of religious fervor during the height of the Cold War. It was a dark and scary period, as people feared that a nuclear holocaust could be unleashed at any moment. As is usually the case in such dark times, religion was a great source of comfort.

Although most Americans approve or do not care about the statement, there have been any dissenters. People state that the placement of such a motto on government currency is a clear violation of the separation of church and state. Interestingly enough, in official defense of the phrase, the notion of "ceremonial deism" has been invoked. This involves the argument that vague references to a higher deity are allowed as long as all distinct religious affiliations have been removed. Thus, one can speak of God as long as they are not too specific as to the nature of the deity that has been invoked. Every American is free to create their own interpretation and view the invoked deity through their own theological lens.

At any rate, the separation of church and state was championed by Thomas Jefferson, who would go on to be elected America's third president. He would serve from 1801 to 1809 and helped ensure that the trend for the separation of church and state, which he had long envisioned, would continue.

Chapter 11: Christian Conformists and Conspiracies of the 19th Century

The 19th century was most certainly a century of change, as advancements in science, technology, and cultural understanding were made and shaped the latest strains of religious thought. After all, the 19th century was the century that saw the rise of Charles Darwin and the subsequent atheistic beliefs that would follow. Atheists sought to describe the advent of the universe as the product of natural evolution with no intelligent designer behind it, although it must be noted that Darwin never saw himself as an atheist.

The changes in mainstream thought in the 19th century continue to have ramifications on religious discourse to this very day. Even though not everyone believed in evolution back then (and even today), the 19th century promoted a strong brand of Christian secularism. Christianity was viewed in more symbolic and general terms than it had been in the past.

To be sure, there were still plenty of literalists out there, but in the 19th century, secularization first received widespread popularity. After the end of the Napoleonic Wars in 1815, much of the Christian West changed. Protestant lands in the European north and in North America began to lead the way for even more religious reforms.

In that same fateful year of 1815, the first evangelical bishop was appointed in North America. Evangelicals of this period began to turn away from theological debates and religious doctrine and focused more on ways to improve society. In contrast to Martin Luther's dislike of the emphasis on "works," this new strain of evangelicals had come to agree with Apostle James's words all those years ago when he emphatically stated that "faith without works is dead."

Evangelical Christians of the 19th century led the charge in the establishment of charitable works, such as orphanages, schools, aid for the poor, and treatment for the sick. These efforts would be crystalized by the formation of the Peace Society in 1828, which championed many of these causes. It seems that there was a decision to move away from theological debates and instead lead by example.

Even more imperative, many came to believe that it was incumbent upon Christians to make Earth just a little bit more like heaven. Christians needed to work to establish the kingdom of heaven on Earth in the present so that it would be ready and waiting for Christ when he returned. These were some pretty lofty goals for the 19th-century church, but many were eager to see them fulfilled.

Some were more militant than others, with some even creating their own "army." This was the case with British evangelical William Booth, who founded the Salvation Army. The Salvation Army was a charitable organization dedicated to the uplifting of the poor and the betterment of society. Taking on the trappings of a literal military host, to this day, the bell ringers of the Salvation Army ask for donations on street corners and can sometimes be seen decked out in military-style uniforms.

At this point, North America, in particular, had a peculiar problem. Although good works were being carried out, even the most obtuse of evangelical Christians could not fail to recognize the terrible bad works that were afoot in the Western world in the form of slavery. If Christ was going to come, they reasoned he most certainly would not return to a country practicing slavery.

Soon enough, evangelicals led the cause to abolish slavery once and for all. British evangelicals succeeded in this goal before their American counterparts. Britain had abolished slavery throughout its empire (including in Canada) by the 1830s. It would take America another thirty years to do the same thing. The interesting thing about the evangelical movement and the desire to abolish slavery is that sentiments were divided in America.

In Britain, the evangelicals presented a united front in standing up to slavery. But over in America, the Northern evangelicals and the Southern evangelicals were split over the issue. While the North churned out an endless stream of Christian abolitionists, Southerners, who were deeply wedded to the slave culture, were much more hesitant to get involved. Even after the Civil War came to a close in 1865 and slavery was abolished, a palpable split would remain between Northern and Southern Christians.

Charles Darwin's work *On the Origin of Species* had been published in 1859, enticing many Christians to give up on Christianity altogether. For the first time, many considered an alternative explanation for their reason for being. Some began to speculate that life was just the product of a natural evolutionary process from an otherwise eternal universe.

At any rate, both non-Christians and even some Christians were captivated by Charles Darwin's research. However, a rather dangerous philosophical belief (at least in regards to religion) arose from his scientific explanations. Rather than depending upon a benevolent God, Darwin described all of life as a product of the environment and that the success of one organism over another was the result of "survival of the fittest."

According to Darwin, one's environment and conditions for living are what shape and hone any given organism, and it was merely the game of survival that makes species what they are. This mindset led to something called social Darwinism. And the notion of social Darwinism would create some very dangerous ideas. With God taken out of the equation, some would take Darwin's observations of "survival of the fittest" and work them into an extreme ideology that asserted only the fittest should be allowed to survive.

Of course, these ideas are quite contrary to the old Christian ideals of charity and caring for the sick and poor. The social Darwinists, like some puffed-up lions prowling the savannah, would take it upon themselves to pounce on the afflicted, and rather than help them, they actively worked on finishing them off. It sounds like the plot of some disturbing dystopian novel in which folks of the future fling wheelchair-bound patients off cliffs simply because they were not "fit" enough.

The ugly side of humanity surfaced as a direct result of Darwin's theories. It must be noted that there is no proof that Darwin himself supported social Darwinism. For the most part, Darwin applied his theories strictly to the biological level. Others, most notably fellow biologist and philosopher Herbert Spencer, took the leap and applied it to social constructs on a massive scale.

Nevertheless, Charles Darwin's findings inspired many to turn away from the Christian faith. Further scientific and even archaeological discoveries also delivered blows to the religion. The discovery of dinosaur bones and the development of carbon dating suggested that Earth had existed for billions of years (rather than the ten thousand or so years conceived by many theologians), which would confuse and dismay many believers.

It suddenly seemed as if there was a whole epoch of history for which the Bible did not account. Nevertheless, as Apostle John said in the Gospel of John, if everything Christ did (let alone everything God did before the creation of humanity) had been recorded in the scripture, the Bible would have to be much bigger to contain all of the information.

Having said that, most Christians today accept that Earth is indeed billions of years old and acknowledge the existence of dinosaurs. These Christians tend to look at the scripture as something that was compiled as a need-to-know basis for humanity. Human beings did not need to know about dinosaurs, so the Bible did not mention it. Others view the stories in the Bible as stories and not truths; for instance, they don't believe Adam and Eve were necessarily the first humans. Instead, they believe the stories impart important truths to apply to their lives. In the case of Adam and Eve, God will grant good and wondrous things if one only believes and follows his instructions.

In this sense, Christians have come to put a laser focus on God's plan of salvation and how it directly reflects on them. They accept that there are many things that we do not know and might never know. Yet, at the same time, they believe we do not need to know everything. As many mainline Christians today might tell you, all you need to know is Jesus!

One last interesting note about the whole debate between Christians and dinosaurs is the arguments that some theologians have made suggesting that the Bible is not wrong. It is just the age-old interpretation of the creation story that is at odds with what the scripture is actually telling us. Contrary to popular interpretation, the Book of Genesis does not start off with God creating Earth from scratch.

If one pays close attention, the arrival of humans in Genesis seems to start somewhere in the middle of the creation story rather than at the very beginning. Yes, the narrative does start off with the words "In the beginning," but by the time the narrative shifts to the creation of human beings, distinct clues are dropped that indicate Earth (as in prehistoric times) already existed before humanity came on the scene.

In the first verse of Genesis, scripture tells us very simply that, "In the beginning, God created the heavens and the Earth" (Genesis 1:1). This is in reference to the very beginning, as in the big bang beginning. But in the second verse, one can sense that the narrative has jumped forward in time because it goes on to say, "Now the Earth was formless and empty, darkness was over the surface of the deep, and the Spirit of God was hovering over the waters" (Genesis 1:2).

It seems like there is a gap in time between the initial creation of the heavens (the universe) and Earth. Those who point out this apparent gap in the biblical timeline have become proponents of the aptly named "gap theory." This theory insists that Genesis is adequately relating to how the material universe, including Earth, was created. They saw there was a gap between the initial creation and the later establishment of humans.

That gap very well could have spanned billions of years, during which time dinosaurs and other prehistoric creatures roamed Earth. Most scientists believe that the great extinction event that killed the dinosaurs was likely from a comet or asteroid that smashed into the planet. This asteroid would have sent up huge clouds of dust and blocked out the sun. And just as the Bible puts it, there would have been "darkness over the surface of the deep."

So, gap theory proponents suggest there was a tremendous gap between the first verse of Genesis, which established creation, and the second verse, which mentions that Earth was shrouded in darkness. If prehistoric life had previously been annihilated in an extinction-level event, then the creation that God began in the second verse was not the first creation of life on Earth but rather the recreation of life, which included the advent of humanity.

It is an interesting theory since the subsequent verses of Genesis talk about what one would expect to transpire in a world recovering from asteroid bombardment. Earth was shrouded in darkness, and God said, "Let there be light." The clouds finally parted, and life began to form once again on Earth.

If we were to ask our gap theory proponents why God did not mention the four billion years of history that occurred between Genesis 1 and 2, they would most likely say we do not need to know about it.

At any rate, whether you believe in the accuracy of the Bible or adhere to an Abrahamic faith or not, it is fun to see just how flexible the scripture and faith can be. Time and time again, from Friedrich Nietzsche to Charles Darwin, there have been those who have speculated that Christianity might soon be relegated to the dustbin as an obsolete relic of the past.

Yet, time and time again, we are surprised by just how adaptable the Christian faith is. If major world religions are gauged on their theological ability to adapt, Christianity almost always seems to come out on top, astonishing everyone with its incredible resilience and adaptability. Part of this can be attributed to the fervent love and devotion Christians have for their faith.

In addition to the discovery of dinosaurs and the advent of carbon dating, there was quite a fervor when the *Epic of Gilgamesh* was discovered buried in the dust of ancient Mesopotamia (modern-day Iraq). The *Epic of Gilgamesh* has a flood story that seems to predate Moses's description of the flood yet is strikingly similar in both detail and scope.

Many have since wondered if this was the source of Moses's account. But even if the stories are similar, it could very well be that both accounts are different versions of the same event. It does not necessarily mean the flood did not happen. Moses was just given a different variation of the same account, which would make sense since he would have written about it long after the flood had occurred (if he wrote it down at all, as modern scholars believe the early books of the Old Testament were written long after his death).

Such a thing is not so surprising when one considers the fact that the father of the Hebrew people—Abraham—originally hailed from Mesopotamia before he was led to the promised land of Israel. Abraham predated Moses's compiling of Genesis, and he was likely aware of a flood story, although, during his life, it might have been passed down as an oral legend.

Rabbinic scholar Robert Wexler believes this to be the case. In a commentary dating back to 2001, he went on the record to state, "The most likely assumption we can make is that both Genesis and Gilgamesh drew their material from a common tradition about the flood that existed in Mesopotamia. These stories then diverged in the retelling."

At any rate, there were plenty of happenings in the 19th century that caused some Christians to begin to doubt their faith. Others found new and intriguing ways to continue to support their beliefs.

Chapter 12: Christianity since the 20th Century and Beyond

At the outset of the 20th century, Christian believers all over the world were hopeful that the new century would bring forth a golden age of renewed faith in Christianity. Despite the fact that the 19th century began a lasting trend of secularism, many were upbeat at the prospect of bringing "the light of Christianity" to all corners of the globe.

Many preachers spread the message that Christianity had reached its "final phase" and that, as soon as the gospel reached the whole world, Christ's return would be imminent. And for those who leaned more toward a social gospel of uplifting the everyday lives of their fellow humans, it was believed that Western Christianity, coupled with notions of democracy and a proactive progressive civilization, would naturally promote peaceful and justice-loving societies all over the world.

From our vantage point, well over one hundred years later, it is easy for us to scoff at such notions. Even with the most cursory examinations of a history book, we know that the 20th century was one of the most violent and disastrous centuries humanity has ever known. Rather than the light of Christianity bringing universal love and brotherhood and peace descending like a dove, the people living in the 20th century suffered two devastating world wars, international terrorism, and the advent of world-destroying nuclear weapons.

But as 1899 rolled over to the year 1900, Christians had no idea what lay in store, and many were quite hopeful that technological progress, coupled with renewed Christian evangelism, would bring about peace and prosperity. This was the general view among Protestants, and the Catholic view was very similar.

In 1905, Pope Pius X famously declared, "The civilization of the world is Christian ... The more completely Christian it is, the more true, more lasting and more productive of genuine fruit it is." Pope Pius insisted that society was on a wayward trend for the better but that the Catholic Church needed to take a more proactive stance for a "more completely Christian" transformation. Both Protestants and Catholics were hedging their bets that the 20th century would indeed be a Christian one.

The First World War would shatter much of those assumptions, as strategic alliances led practically the entire planet to war. World War One was triggered by a Serbian nationalist who assassinated a visiting archduke from Austria. Austria-Hungary was understandably incensed at this turn of events and issued a series of draconian demands.

The Serbs had no intention of meeting all of the demands, some of which were absurd. Austria used this rejection as an excuse to declare war on Serbia. Russia, which was allied with Serbia, then declared war on Austria-Hungary. Austria's ally Germany declared war on Russia. Britain and France then declared war on Germany. And the next thing anyone knew, just about all of the major world powers had declared war on each other over an incident that should have been an isolated event, although other factors were certainly at play.

Young men all over the world paid the price. They were sent to the trenches to be gassed and riddled with machine gun bullets. Many wondered not only what the point of the war was but also what was the point of life and their faith in God. Such questions tend to arise when change comes so rapidly and drastically. Chaos does seem to either drive people away from their faith or drive them closer to it.

Some instances of the revival of the Christian faith can be traced to the onset of World War One. Considering how easily the world had descended into an apocalyptic situation, it is understandable why previous Christian notions of universal peace under Christ were shattered. Perhaps most peculiar is the fact that mainstream Christians even had such a mindset in the first place.

The Christian New Testament was written in the tumultuous time of the 1st century when Jesus and his early disciples lived under the oppression of Roman occupation. The views of the early Christians were that before things got better, they would get a whole lot worse. And although it was agreed that peace would triumph in the end, much of their ideas of the future had more to do with Armageddon than peaceful coexistence among the nations.

Perhaps the disappointments of the breakdown of international peace and order shifted the Christian mindset back toward this old Christian worldview. And in many ways, it has been stuck there ever since. You are indeed more likely to hear Christians today speaking that the end is near and that they are "ready for the Rapture."

The world wars shattered the notion that Christianity would be the glue that would hold the international world order together, and there was a great return to the apocalyptic outlook. Immediately after World War One, many "old world" orders were destroyed. Both the Austro-Hungarian Empire and the Ottoman Empire fell apart. The loss of the Austro-Hungarian Empire redrew the borders of Europe. Perhaps even more importantly, the loss of the Ottoman juggernaut dramatically refashioned the geographical areas of the Middle East and North Africa.

The destruction of the Ottoman Empire would create the British mandate over Palestine. Palestine, or, as it is otherwise known, "Ersatz Israel" or the "Land of Israel," is the land talked about in the Bible. Western Christians did not have control over the Holy Land since the Crusades. And now they were back.

Prior to this event, it was popular for Christians to believe that God's covenant had shifted to the Christian Church. In the Old Testament of the Bible, God is said to have a covenant with the land of Israel, but something happened in the interim, with Israel becoming largely irrelevant. After the British successfully seized this land from the Ottomans, the development of the modern nation-state of Israel began. The Christians' view began to shift, and prophecy prognosticators began to again look toward the land of Israel as being pivotal to God's plan.

In the meantime, Europe was severely shaken by World War Two. The conflict was a terrible one, but one group whose suffering is often overlooked is the German Church. Early on, German nationalists attempted to co-opt German Christians by promoting a blend of Christianity that was linked to the German state. Many fell for this redressing of the church, but by the mid-1930s, when extreme reforms called for radical changes in Christian ideology, such as dropping the Old Testament and even the epistles of Apostle Paul, German Christians finally (albeit much too late) tried to take action.

Religious dissidents in Germany formed what was known as the Confessing Church, which sought to uphold the word of God as sovereign no matter what Hitler or his cronies told anyone. These efforts were crystalized in the 1934 Barmen Declaration, which officially condemned what the German state was doing and sought to reaffirm the traditional beliefs of the church. The declaration declared, in part, "We reject the false doctrine [that nationalism can dictate to the churches] as though the Church were permitted to abandon the form of its message and order to its own pleasure or to changes in prevailing ideological and political convictions."

By then, the German state was firmly in the hands of the extremists, and it did not take much to send any dissidents to the concentration camps. In a short period of time, well over seven hundred German pastors who protested what was happening in their country were seized. One of the loudest German voices to stand against what the government was doing was Christian theologian Dietrich Bonhoeffer.

Although Bonhoeffer faced a fate worse than death, he refused to stand down. He was ultimately rounded up and liquidated by the German authorities. Those who were not arrested were repeatedly threatened with imprisonment and far worse until they meekly put their heads down, caved to the pressure, and kept their mouths shut. As much as we might want to condemn these Germans for not standing up to their government, there are likely plenty of people today who might cave to the demands of a totalitarian regime. It can be hard to put yourself in someone else's shoes. This is not to excuse the German Church's choice to back down in the face of aggression, but it does explain why most Christians ended up acquiescing so easily.

And speaking of totalitarian regimes, in the Soviet Union, Christianity faced a surprising turn of events. Since the days of Karl Marx, the communists derided religion as nothing more than the opiate of the masses, the carrot that was strung above the heads of the poor and weary so that they would keep moving forward and keep punching in their time clock until the day they died.

The communists taught the people that religion was a delusion and was used to keep people in line with the promise of a false reward at the end of their lives. As such, it should not be surprising to learn that when communists took over Russia in 1917, they began persecuting the Russian Church. What is surprising to learn is that during the darkest days of World War Two, totalitarian dictator Joseph Stalin decided to reopen the church!

As the Russians were being beaten back by the Germans, it was feared that a march on Moscow was imminent. Stalin was crafty enough to realize that the Russians needed a powerful symbol, a unifying force to hold them all together. Stalin, who had at one time considered becoming a priest, knew the only thing that could unite Russians was religion.

Stalin not only reopened churches but also actively encouraged the people's belief in Christianity as a means of holding his people and ultimately the Soviet Union together. His bid seemed to work well enough, as the average Russian seemed to view the protection of their homeland and way of life as something more akin to a holy war and a fight for their survival.

On the heels of World War Two, Christian theologians latched on to what they perceived to be a portent of biblical proportions. After the war came to a close, the United States and the United Nations facilitated Israel becoming a nation again in 1948. At this point, one can clearly mark the shift in Christian beliefs regarding the "end times." Apocalyptic prophecies were once again given a Middle Eastern background, with Christians beginning to foresee an imminent "end times" showdown in Israel.

It was proclaimed that enemy nations would march on Israel right before the Rapture. Israel's destruction would only be prevented by the return of Christ himself. The fact that Israel wasn't even considered in end-times prophecies for hundreds of years is rather telling. It demonstrates just how elastic some of the interpretations of scripture and apocalyptic prophecies can be.

As it pertains to the Catholic Church, the Vatican seemed to come out stronger after the war. This is surprising, considering the still lingering controversy over how the Catholic Church interacted with Italy's fascist government of Benito Mussolini. The church has been criticized for its perceived cooperation, but in truth, the church made more efforts than perhaps any other institution behind the walls of fascism to actually do something about what was happening in the country.

The church worked to actively save many from the horrors of the Holocaust. Even so, many might have predicted that the Catholic Church might splinter or become irrelevant after the war, with the pope being viewed as a compromised political tool of despots. But in reality, the Catholic Church became stronger and managed to retake its traditional role as an international arbiter.

The Vatican regained its status as a nation-state, and the pope was again the potentate. He just so happened to have the support of over a billion faithful Catholics all over the world. Then there came the watershed moment of "Vatican II." This ecumenical council kicked off in September 1962, with subsequent meetings taking place all the way until the year 1965. The council called for the Catholic Church to take on a much more active role in world affairs, among other things.

And considering the efforts of popes like John Paul II (who is credited with being instrumental in bringing communism to an end) and the present (at least as of this writing) Pope Francis, the Catholic Church has largely followed this pattern of positioning itself as an arbiter for world dialogue and change. One of the most pivotal results of Vatican II was the voiced determination to end the long-standing antagonism that had developed between Catholics and Protestants.

Since the Reformation, the two branches of Christianity have often been at each other's throats. However, Vatican II decided it was time to cease competing with the Protestants and try and cooperate with them as much as would be feasible.

In the United States, some mainline Protestants and Catholics would embrace something that would become known as the Social Gospel. This movement was similar to what had occurred previously in the 19th century, as Christianity was again used in the social uplifting of humanity. But unlike its predecessor, this new variant had a much more urgent call to action. It was closely intertwined with popular social movements, such as the civil rights movement and the feminist movement.

The Social Gospel stressed that the time to act to make the world a better place was now and urged folks to step out of the churches and into the streets to take a more active role in shaping the society in which they lived. Those who adhered to the Social Gospel would often stand in sharp contrast with the more conservative brand of evangelical Christianity, which, in the West, was being led by the likes of Billy Graham and other similar firebrand preachers.

Billy Graham was not as likely to preach on immediate social change as he was to warn people that the end was near. Billy Graham came up with a very resonant message: the end times were fast approaching. He often galvanized the masses to convert through the powerful imagery that he conveyed.

Of course, Billy Graham was not the first preacher to convey that an apocalypse was nigh. But considering the advent of nuclear weapons and the fact that, by the early 1960s, the United States and Russia had amassed enough nuclear armaments to blow up the whole planet with the push of a button, Billy Graham's message became palpable. It seemed as if an uncontrollable and unrelenting Armageddon really was about to blow up in everyone's faces.

The idea of a nuclear Armageddon was quite influential on Christian thought. It really cannot be overemphasized how powerful these world events were in shaping the notion among Christians that the end was near. Such things could have been suggested in the past, but the threat seemed much more realistic during the Cold War. Even today, when the brink of nuclear war occasionally raises its head, there will inevitably be many preachers who speak up to declare that the long prophesized "end of days" is about to commence.

As an indication of how powerful this "end times" imagery is, Christian theologian Hal Lindsey wrote a book about how he thought the end would play out called *The Late Great Planet Earth*. The book came out in 1970 and was an immediate bestseller. Rather than losing relevance, the book is still popular to this day, and Hal Lindsey himself still claims it to be an accurate portrayal of what might happen. The only difference is the level of "imminence" of the end.

Preaching of the end times has not really abated much; however, the goalposts keep shifting. In truth, the Christian Church has been looking for the end to come since Jesus first preached that the "kingdom of heaven is at hand" in the 1st century. The early church was waiting for the end times two thousand years ago, and Christians are still waiting today. Although the Bible itself suggests that the end will come, it does not set dates.

When asked about when the final trumpet might sound, Jesus declared, "Only the Father knows." As Matthew 24:36 tells us, "But nobody knows when that day or hour will come, not the heavenly angels and not the Son. Only the Father knows."

The scripture also states that, to God, "a day is like a thousand years, and a thousand years are like a day" (2nd Peter 3:8), leading some modern-day preachers to quip that two thousand years is nothing in the grand scheme of things. Evangelist Jesse Duplantis is fond of brushing off any notion that the Second Coming is taking too long by stating that, from God's perspective, only a weekend has passed since the resurrection. For him and many other preachers, there is no delay—God is still right on schedule.

Another great shift in Christianity in the 20th century that cannot be overlooked is Pentecostalism. The Pentecostal faith champions a direct, personal connection to God, which is often demonstrated by means of expressive religious experiences, such as lifting hands, falling down, and speaking in what has been termed "tongues."

Pentecostals believe that when they are filled with the Holy Spirit and make a direct connection to the divine, these experiences occur. Pentecostalism began as a fringe movement in the early 20th century but has since become one of the most popular and growing brands of Christianity. To gauge just how popular Pentecostalism has become, all one has to do is flip on Christian television.

Christian TV, by and large, is dominated by promoters of the Pentecostal faith. Billy Graham may have been a firebrand Baptist who braved the airwaves, but today, almost every TV evangelist you see is likely of the Pentecostal faith. Pentecostal beliefs are also rapidly spreading all over Latin America.

Practitioners of the Catholic faith are now finding stiff competition among Pentecostal believers in Latin America. In Brazil, for example, it is said that over 16 percent of the population is Pentecostal. As these Christian movements continue to grow, we can be sure that the future will provide even more enrichment and development of the Christian faith.

Conclusion:
The Reason for the Season and the Reason We Keep Believing

It is fairly safe to say, now that some two thousand years have gone by, that the Christian faith has stood the test of time. Although its practitioners have adapted some of their practices and views over the centuries, the faith itself is still going strong. Christianity not only has the most adherents by sheer numbers but is also one of the few religions that actually gets celebrated by those who do not even believe in it.

If one would like to see evidence of the global dominance of Christianity, all one has to do is consider the celebration of Christmas. Almost two hundred countries today celebrate Christmas.

Although one might be tempted to discount the significance of such a thing and suggest that it is just the influence of Western commercialism at work, such a notion does not adequately explain the pure joy with which Christmas is approached and celebrated. And whether we realize it or not, the themes of Christ and Christianity have permeated even the most supposedly secular renderings of the holiday.

Just take, for example, the tale of "Frosty the Snowman." This is a perfectly secular tale with no religious connotations whatsoever, right? It speaks of a snowman who was "magically" brought to life (the immaculate conception) one day. The snowman gained a following because of his kindness and pureness of heart (he was a jolly, happy soul). In the 1969 animated movie, the snowman perished in a heroic act of self-sacrifice.

A girl was freezing to death in the cold, so Frosty took her to a warm greenhouse even though he knew he would melt. He died so others could live. The girl is then found crying her eyes out (just like Mary Magdalene crying in Christ's tomb), only for the benevolent, fatherly figure of Santa to show up and bring Frosty the Snowman back to life (the resurrection). The kids rejoice but are sad to see Frosty fly off with Santa to the North Pole (the ascension). But even so, Frosty "waved good-bye, saying, 'Don't you cry—I'll be back again someday!'"

Now, perhaps this silly analogy might provoke some laughs. But in all seriousness, one cannot help but be astonished by how the themes of Christ and Christianity seem almost inescapable as it pertains to Christmas, even when we try to suppress or avoid them. Perhaps they are just so ingrained in our hearts and souls that even when a secular writer is tasked with writing a Christmas tale about a snowman, they somehow can't help subconsciously giving that frosty fellow some rather Christ-like attributes!

And there has to be a reason for that. The reason for the season has always been Jesus Christ and the followers of the Christian faith, who have long kept Christian beliefs front and center in the consciousness of humanity as a whole.

Here's another book by Enthralling History that you might like

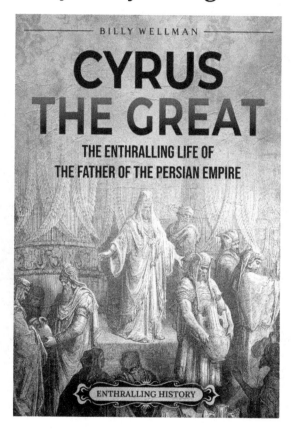

Free limited time bonus

Stop for a moment. We have a free bonus set up for you. The problem is this: we forget 90% of everything that we read after 7 days. Crazy fact, right? Here's the solution: we've created a printable, 1-page pdf summary for this book that you're reading now. All you have to do to get your free pdf summary is to go to the following website: **https://livetolearn.lpages.co/enthrallinghistory/**

Once you do, it will be intuitive. Enjoy, and thank you!

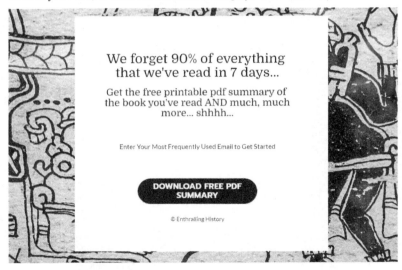

Appendix A: Further Reading and Reference

Holland, Tom. *Dominion: How the Christian Revolution Remade the World.* 2019.

MacCulloch, Diarmaid. *A History of Christianity: The First Three Thousand Years.* 2009.

Mullin, Bruce Robert. *A Short World History of Christianity.* 2006.

Shelley, Bruce. *Christian Theology in Plain Language.* 1982.

Ware, Kalistos. *The Orthodox Church.* 1963.

Made in the USA
Middletown, DE
28 February 2023

25900854R00066